Iris A n

PRAISE FOR *ACTIVE HOPE*

"The response to the profound crisis we are living thro
urgent, appropriate, and driven by possibilities. It mu
in compassion and a focus on bringing us together in su
can create anything we set our minds to. It is to this chal
and Chris turn their minds here, and I for one am deep
wisdom they offer us."

— Rob Hopkins, cofounder of the Transition Network and author of
The Transition Handbook: From Oil Dependency to Local Resilience

"Words cannot fully express my gratitude for this book's appearance at
this time. With ancient wisdom, deep compassion, and years of experience, Joanna and Chris guide us through this perilous time, not that we
might succeed in saving the world, but that we might consciously choose
to participate, no matter the outcome. This is the path of right action
and right relationship, where joy and peace are available independent
of what's going on around us. May we take this beautiful book into our
hearts that we may each find the path with heart."

— Margaret J. Wheatley, author of *Perseverance*,
Leadership and the New Science, and other books

"I loved this book. Its brilliance lies in the way it skillfully addresses and
transforms the major limiting beliefs that hold people back from whole-
hearted social action, which at its heart requires that 'active hope' be sustained. It then gently, but inexorably, invites us to participate in the great
adventure of our time of changing the world. Joanna and Chris have laid
out a twenty-first-century spiritual path for deep and soul-filled social
action. Read it and be nourished!"

— David Gershon, author of
Social Change 2.0: A Blueprint for Reinventing Our World
and codirector of Empowerment Institute's School
for Transformative Social Change

"Our species is going through a collective Dark Night of the Soul. The
authors call this the 'Great Turning,' and they provide ample nourishment in the form of concepts and practices that are sure to help us
navigate our way. This book is a lucid, timely, practical, and very-much-
needed gift. With the guidance offered, we learn how to stay true to our

vocations so that neither fear nor despair nor uncertainty nor opposition defeats us. A welcome manual for navigating the Dark Night of our species. Most welcome!"

— Matthew Fox, author of
The Hidden Spirituality of Men and *Christian Mystics*

"Joanna Macy is one of the great teachers of this age. What a delight, then, to read her latest work, written with medical doctor and addiction specialist Chris Johnstone. *Active Hope* helps us to gaze unflinchingly at the horrors that confront us, to honor the pain we feel for our world, and to allow the truth to strengthen rather than paralyze us. It's hard to think of a more important task than to empower us ordinary folk with tools that allow us to engage with the monumental challenges that confront us — tools that nourish our creativity and bolster our confidence and resilience. If you want to serve the living Earth but don't know how, if you feel overwhelmed by the magnitude of the task ahead, if you want to find the part that only you can play in the 'great work,' please read this book."

— John Seed, OAM, founder of the Rainforest Information Centre

"*Active Hope* is the Great Turning's New Testament. It is that rarity in the literature of self-help that unfolds as if organically in prose that, like the best sacred writing, induces the mind shift it encourages. Here are the unflinching diagnosis and prognosis and widely tested protocol for self-healing and lifesaving that can help a critical mass of us to recommit to learning, living, and acting effectively on behalf of Earth's beleaguered human and natural communities. *Active Hope* is laced with vivid analogies, anecdotes, and opportunities to envision the world we would wish to leave our children and grandchildren. I began reading it because I was asked to; I kept reading because I needed to. For all who are worried for the success of their work in the sustainability, environmental, new economy, or social justice movements, this book will be both a guide and a medicine."

— Ellen LaConte, author of *Life Rules: Why So Much Is Going Wrong Everywhere at Once and How Life Teaches Us to Fix It*

"*Active Hope* offers a way of living creatively in a time of great challenges, a time when humanity is threatened by ecological, social, and economic breakdown. Joanna and Chris show us how to frame our actions so that we can help contribute to the global movement for a better, more equitable, and ecologically balanced world. This is a juicy, creative, and powerful book."

— Maddy Harland, editor of *Permaculture* magazine,
www.permaculture.co.uk

"Active hope is something you choose, we're told in this powerful, inspiring book. Joanna Macy and Chris Johnstone offer not just an antidote to despair but a new lease on life, a way to do our part to heal our broken world. *Active Hope* is one of the most important works to appear in years and should be read by everyone young and old who cares about what is happening to our world. Pass it on and join the campaign to spread hope! It's never too late to make a difference."

— Rev. John Dear, lecturer, activist, and author of *Living Peace*,
The Questions of Jesus, *Transfiguration*, *Put Down Your Sword*,
The God of Peace, and *Seeds of Nonviolence*

"There are few guides in our world that are as trustworthy and brilliant as Joanna Macy! In *Active Hope*, she and Chris Johnstone give us not only some very good analysis but also good responses and practices — in a very readable and engaging style."

— Fr. Richard Rohr, OFM, Center for Action and Contemplation,
Albuquerque, New Mexico

"Before turning these pages, I was experiencing the total darkness of a midnight depression. I felt incapable of thinking through, much less taking, a necessary step in my life. Then I opened to the pages of Joanna and Chris's exercise 'The Bodhisattva Perspective.' Within minutes, I saw an otherwise inconceivable hope in the interconnected life I had chosen. It was a simple miracle of transformed consciousness. *Active Hope* is not just a book but a gateway to transformation."

— Jim Douglass, author of *JFK and the Unspeakable*

"Renowned Earth elder Joanna Macy has long exemplified what it means to live a life of spiritual activism and courageous compassion. Here, with her colleague Chris Johnstone, she offers the essential guidebook for everyone awakening to both the perils and potentials of our planetary moment. In this clearly written and compelling manual of cultural transformation, Joanna and Chris guide us to find hope where we might least have thought to look — within our own hearts and souls, and in our interdependence with all life — and then to boldly act on that hope as visionary artisans of life-enhancing cultures. To the future beings of the twenty-second century, *Active Hope* might turn out to be the most important book written in the twenty-first."

— Bill Plotkin, author of *Soulcraft* and *Nature and the Human Soul*

"Given the state of the world, how do we find a truly sane, effective, and life-affirming response? Joanna Macy, one of the true wisdom voices of our age, has devoted her life to helping people find their resilience, their creativity, and their passion while living with their eyes and hearts open. Her work is powerful, needed, and lifesaving. If you have despaired for our world, and if you love life, *Active Hope* will be for you an extraordinary blessing."

— John Robbins, author of *Diet for a New America*
and *The Food Revolution*

"We belong to the Earth, and our precious living world is in crisis. More than any book I've read, *Active Hope* shows us the true dimensions of this crisis, and the way our heart and actions can be part of the great turning toward healing. Please read this book and share it with others — for your own awakening, for our children, and for our future."

— Tara Brach, PhD, author of *Radical Acceptance*

"This is a powerful book to read in these dark times. Written with wisdom and passion, it is about balanced compassion and hope, love and strength, and the will to make a difference. *Active Hope* is a brilliant guide to sanity and love."

— Roshi Joan Halifax, abbot of the Upaya Zen Center

ACTIVE
HOPE

ACTIVE HOPE

How to Face
the Mess We're in
without Going Crazy

JOANNA MACY &
CHRIS JOHNSTONE

New World Library
Novato, California

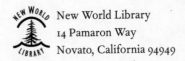

New World Library
14 Pamaron Way
Novato, California 94949

Interior illustrations on page 39 by Dori Midnight and on pages 154 and 156 by Dave Baines
Text design by Tona Pearce Myers
Cover design by Tracy Cunningham

Library of Congress Cataloging-in-Publication Data
Macy, Joanna, date.
Active hope : how to face the mess we're in without going crazy / Joanna Macy and Chris Johnstone.
    p.   cm.
Includes bibliographical references and index.
ISBN 978-1-57731-972-6 (pbk. : alk. paper)
1. Social change—Environmental aspects. 2. Social change—Psychological aspects. 3. Social change—Religious aspects. 4. Environmental psychology. I. Johnstone, Chris, date. II. Title.
HM856.M33 2012
303.4—dc23   2011049855

First printing, March 2012
ISBN 978-1-57731-972-6
Printed in the USA on 100% postconsumer-waste recycled paper

 New World Library is proud to be a Gold Certified Environmentally Responsible Publisher. Publisher certification awarded by Green Press Initiative. www.greenpressinitiative.org

20 19 18 17 16 15 14 13 12 11

This book is dedicated
to the flourishing of life
on this rare and wondrous planet.

Contents

Acknowledgments

We begin with gratitude, remembering the words of Thich Nhat Hanh: "If you are a poet, you will see clearly that there is a cloud floating in this sheet of paper. Without a cloud, there will be no rain; without rain, the trees cannot grow: and without trees, we cannot make paper." So it is with this book. Without all those who've played supporting roles, it would simply not be here. So our thanks extends to all who have helped, particularly:

The core team involved in its production. Early on in our book-writing journey, we were joined by two people who understood what we were setting out to do and who were with us in this purpose: our agent, Suresh Ariaratnam, and our editor, Jason Gardner. What a relief to have you alongside us. Thank you. We're grateful to Dori Midnight for the wonderful spiral illustration in chapter 2, to Dave Baines for the two intriguing spirals of time in chapter 8, and to all at New World Library for the different roles they've played, particularly Mimi Kusch for copy editing, Monique Muhlenkamp for publicity, Tona Pearce Myers for the interior design, Tracy Cunningham for the cover design, and Munro Magruder for marketing. We would like also to thank the many who have inspired us, particularly those we've quoted, such as John Robbins, John Seed, Rebecca Solnit, Tom Atlee, Nelson Mandela, and the late Arne Naess and Elise Boulding.

The many friends and family who have supported us while writing.

Joanna's husband, Fran, supported us right from the beginning. We have felt him as a powerful ally, even after his death in 2009. Joanna particularly thanks her assistant Anne Symens-Bucher, her children, Peggy, Jack, and Christopher, and her grandchildren, Julien, Eliza, and Lydia. Chris's wife, Kirsty, encouraged him through writing ups and downs; his mum, Sheila, brother, Dave, and sister, Diana, were great allies too. Hamish Cormack interviewed Chris about each chapter and commented on early drafts. We received invaluable and encouraging feedback from our panel of "test readers," which included Roz Chissick, Marion McCartney, Philip Raby, Helen Moore, Manu Song, Edi Hamilton, Pete Black, Sally Lever, Alex Wildwood, and Sue Mann. Our dear friend Kathleen Sullivan, who has known us both for decades, has been a friend of our writing too, and we thank her.

The countless colleagues in the Work That Reconnects, who have engaged with it as a practice, offered it in places all over the planet, and added their own distinctive contributions. As we take the essence of this approach to wider audiences, we are aware of the ways you have enriched it; our pleasure in your company is boundless.

Introduction

"Dangerous," "frightening," "out of control" — as we go around the room, people are calling out the word or phrase that comes to mind as they complete this sentence: "When I consider the condition of our world, I think things are getting..." Over the last few decades, we've done this process with tens of thousands of people in a wide range of settings. The responses we hear echo survey findings that show high levels of alarm about the future we're heading into.[1]

Such widespread anxiety is well-founded. As our world heats up, deserts expand and extreme weather events become more common. Human population and consumption are increasing at the same time as essential resources, such as freshwater, fish stocks, topsoil, and oil reserves, are in decline. While reversals in the economy have left many feeling desperate about how they're going to manage, trillions of dollars are spent on the making of war.[2] Given these adversities, it is no surprise if we experience a profound loss of confidence in the future. We can no longer take it for granted that the resources we're dependent on — food, fuel, and drinkable water — will be available. We can no longer take it for granted even that our civilization will survive or that conditions on our planet will remain hospitable for complex forms of life.

We are starting out by naming this uncertainty as a pivotal psychological reality of our time. Yet because it is usually considered too depressing to talk about, it tends to remain an unspoken presence at the backs of our minds. Sometimes we're aware of it. We just don't mention it. This blocked communication generates a peril even more deadly, for the greatest danger of our times is the deadening of our response.

We often hear comments such as "Don't go there, it is too depressing" and "Don't dwell on the negative." The problem with this approach is that it closes down our conversations and our thinking. How can we even begin to tackle the mess we're in if we consider it too depressing to think about?

Yet when we do face the mess, when we do let in the dreadful news of multiple tragedies unfolding in our world, it can feel overwhelming. We may wonder whether we can do anything about it anyway.

So this is where we begin — by acknowledging that our times confront us with realities that are painful to face, difficult to take in, and confusing to live with. Our approach is to see this as the starting point of an amazing journey that strengthens us and deepens our aliveness. The purpose of this journey is to find, offer, and receive the gift of Active Hope.

WHAT IS ACTIVE HOPE?

Whatever situation we face, we can choose our response. When facing overwhelming challenges, we might feel that our actions don't count for much. Yet the kind of responses we make, and the degree to which we believe they count, are shaped by the way we think and feel about hope. Here's an example.

Jane cared deeply about the world and was horrified by what she saw happening. She regarded human beings as a lost cause, as so stuck in our destructive ways that she saw the complete wrecking of our world as inevitable. "What's the point of doing anything if it won't change what we're heading for?" she asked.

The word *hope* has two different meanings. The first involves hopefulness, where our preferred outcome seems reasonably likely to happen. If we require this kind of hope before we commit ourselves to an action, our response gets blocked in areas where we don't rate our chances too high. This is what happened for Jane — she felt so hopeless she didn't see the point of even trying to do anything.

The second meaning is about desire. When Jane was asked what she'd like to have happen in our world, without hesitation she described the future she hoped for, the kind of world she longed for so much it hurt. It is this kind of hope that starts our journey — knowing what we hope for and what we'd like, or love, to take place. It is what we do with this hope that really makes the difference. Passive hope is about waiting for external agencies to bring about what we desire. Active Hope is about becoming active participants in bringing about what we hope for.

Active Hope is a practice. Like tai chi or gardening, it is something we *do* rather than *have*. It is a process we can apply to any situation, and it involves three key steps. First, we take a clear view of reality; second, we identify what we hope for in terms of the direction we'd like things to move in or the values we'd like to see expressed; and third, we take steps to move ourselves or our situation in that direction.

Since Active Hope doesn't require our optimism, we can apply it even in areas where we feel hopeless. The guiding impetus is intention; we *choose* what we aim to bring about, act for, or express. Rather than weighing our chances and proceeding only when we feel hopeful, we focus on our intention and let it be our guide.

The Gift Is Both Given and Received

Most books addressing global issues focus on describing either the problems we face or the solutions needed. While we touch on both of these, our focus is on how we strengthen and support our intention to act, so that we can best play our part, whatever that may be, in the healing of our world.

Since we each look out onto a different corner of the planet and bring with us our own particular portfolio of interests, skills, and experience, we are touched by different concerns and called to respond in different ways. The contribution each of us makes to the healing of our world is our gift of Active Hope. The purpose of this book is to strengthen our ability to give the best gift we can: our finest response to the multifaceted crisis of sustainability.

When we become aware of an emergency and rise to the occasion, something powerful gets switched on inside us. We activate our sense of purpose and discover strengths we didn't even know we had. Being able to make a difference is powerfully enlivening; it makes our lives feel more worthwhile. So when we practice Active Hope, we not only give but we receive in so many ways as well. The approach we describe in this book is not about being dutiful or worthy so much as it is about stepping into a state of aliveness that makes our lives profoundly satisfying.

THREE STORIES OF OUR TIME

In any great adventure, there are always obstacles in the way. The first hurdle is just to be aware that we, as a civilization and as a species, are facing a crisis point. When we look at mainstream society, and the priorities expressed or goals pursued, it is hard to see much evidence of this awareness. In the first chapter we try to make sense of the huge gap between the scale of the emergency and the size of the response by describing how our perceptions are shaped by the story we identify with. We describe three stories, or versions of reality, each acting as a lens through which we see and understand what's going on.

In the first of these, Business as Usual, the defining assumption is that there is little need to change the way we live. Economic growth is regarded as essential for prosperity, and the central plot is about getting ahead. The second story, the Great Unraveling, draws attention to the disasters that Business as Usual is taking us toward, as well as those it has already brought about. It is an account, backed by evidence, of the collapse of ecological and social systems, the disturbance of climate, the depletion of resources, and the mass extinction of species.

The third story is held and embodied by those who know the first story is leading us to catastrophe and who refuse to let the second story have the last word. Involving the emergence of new and creative human responses, it is about the epochal transition from an industrial society committed to economic growth to a life-sustaining society committed to the healing and recovery of our world. We call this story the Great Turning. The central plot is finding and offering our gift of Active Hope.

There is no point in arguing about which of these stories is "right." All three are happening. The question is which one we want to put our energy behind. The first chapter is about looking at where we are and choosing the story we want our lives to express. The rest of the book focuses on how we strengthen our capacity to contribute to the Great Turning in the best way we can.

The Spiral of the Work That Reconnects

The journey that begins in chapter 2, and that continues throughout the book, is based on an empowerment process we have offered in workshops for decades. Initially developed by Joanna in the late in 1970s, it evolved and spread, with the vital contribution of a growing number of colleagues. It has been used on every continent except Antarctica, has been conducted in many different languages, and has involved hundreds of thousands of people of different faiths, backgrounds, and age groups. Because this approach helps us restore our sense of connection with the web of life and with one another, it is known as the Work That Reconnects.[3] Through helping us to develop our inner resources and our outer community, it strengthens our capacity to face disturbing information and respond with unexpected resilience. In our experience of doing this work, again and again we've seen energy and commitment mobilized as people rise to their role in the Great Turning.

We've written this book so that you can experience the transformative power of the Work That Reconnects and draw on it to expand your capacity to respond creatively to the crises of our time. The chapters ahead guide you through the four stages of the spiral it moves through: Coming from Gratitude, Honoring Our Pain for the World, Seeing with New Eyes, and Going Forth. The journey through these stages has a strengthening effect that deepens with each repetition.

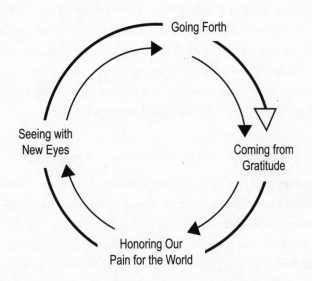

Figure 1. The spiral of the Work That Reconnects

While rich rewards can be reaped while journeying alone, the benefits of the Work That Reconnects grow quickly with company. We encourage you to seek others with whom to read this book or share notes along the way. Bringing our concerns into the open is a key part of facing the mess we are in, though for reasons we will explore, fear often prevents this type of sharing. We will examine what makes it so difficult to talk about our planetary crisis and provide tools that support us in having the empowering conversations our times call for.

We encourage you to gain familiarity with the tools we describe by trying them out. Scattered throughout the book are "Try This" boxes inviting you to experience practices we find valuable both for personal use and in groups.

What We Bring

At the heart of this book is a collaborative model of power based on appreciating how much more we can achieve working together than as separate individuals. The story of our coauthorship is a fine example. The seedling idea sprouted out of a conversation about lessons we had learned from our experience of the Work That Reconnects. What surprised and excited us both was how often, in the many hours of talking that followed, insights would surface that neither of us had received before. While the core framework, concepts, and practices of the Work That Reconnects are well tested, we have been able to enrich, hone, and add to them in ways that bring together a great deal of material not published elsewhere.

There is an old saying that two eyes are better than one, since out of two different perspectives comes the depth of three-dimensional vision. As coauthors we come from different backgrounds, live on different continents, and draw from different sources, all of which has contributed to the rich synergy we have experienced and that is expressed through our writing.

Joanna is a scholar of Buddhism, general systems theory, and deep ecology. She has taught at several universities in the United States and has traveled the world, offering trainings to enliven and empower our responses to planetary crisis. In her early eighties, she lives in Berkeley, California. She has been an activist for more than five decades; is a respected voice in the movements for peace, justice, and ecology; and has either written or cowritten a dozen books, most of which have been translated into other languages.

Chris is a medical doctor who has specialized in the psychology of behavior change, resilience, and recovery from addiction. Living in the United Kingdom, he works as a coach, trains health professionals in behavioral medicine, and has pioneered the role of resilience training in promoting positive mental health. An activist since his teenage years and now in his late forties, he has taught and written about the psychology of sustainability for more than twenty years.

The two of us met in 1989 at a weeklong training led by Joanna in Scotland. Called "The Power of Our Deep Ecology," it was a life-changing event for Chris. We have worked together many times since. This book describes the work we share and cherish. It is offered not as a blueprint solution to our problems but as both a set of practices and insights to draw strength from and as a mythic journey to be transformed by. Rebecca Solnit writes:

> An emergency is a separation from the familiar, a sudden emergence into a new atmosphere, one that often demands we ourselves rise to the occasion.[4]

When we face the mess we're in, we realize that Business as Usual can't go on. What helps us rise to the occasion is experiencing our rootedness in something much larger than ourselves. The poet Rabindranath Tagore expressed this idea in these words:

> The same stream of life that runs through my veins night and day runs through the world.[5]

This is the stream we are following. It points us toward a way of life that enriches rather than depletes our world. It takes us to our gift of Active Hope. When we face the mess we're in by offering this gift, our lives become enriched too.

PART ONE

The Great Turning

CHAPTER ONE

Three Stories of Our Time

*When the stories a society shares are out of tune
with its circumstances, they can become self-limiting,
even a threat to survival. That is our current situation.*

DAVID KORTEN, *The Great Turning*[1]

On May 7, 2001, journalists gathered for a press briefing at the White House. Ari Fleischer, President Bush's press secretary, had nothing to announce that day but invited questions from the assembled crowd. Rising energy costs quickly became the lead topic, with one of the early questions evoking a strong response.

> JOURNALIST: "Does the President believe that, given the amount of energy Americans consume per capita, how much it exceeds any other citizen in any other country in the world, does the President believe we need to correct our lifestyles to address the energy problem?"

> MR. FLEISCHER: "That's a big no. The President believes that it's an American way of life, and that it should be the goal of policy makers to protect the American way of life."[2]

While presidents come and go, Mr. Fleischer's "big no" remains a powerful force in our society. It is the voice that doesn't question the way we live. This conviction grows out of a particular story about how things are in our world. By *story*, we don't mean a work of fiction but rather the way we make sense of the events we see happening.

In this chapter we identify three stories being enacted in our time, as mentioned in the introduction. The first assumes that our society is on the right track and that we can carry on with business as usual. The second reveals the destructive consequences of the business-as-usual mode and the progressive unraveling of our biological, ecological, and social systems. The third is about the groundswell of response to danger and the multifaceted transition to a life-sustaining civilization. Recognizing that we can choose the story we live from can be liberating; finding a good story to take part in adds to our sense of purpose and aliveness. We will explore how these stories shape our response to global crisis.

THE FIRST STORY: BUSINESS AS USUAL

Of the food you've eaten in the last twenty-four hours, how much is based on ingredients produced hundreds, or even thousands, of miles away? For most of us living in industrialized countries, the answer is *lots of it*. The average carrot, head of lettuce, or box of strawberries sold in supermarkets in Iowa, for example, is likely to have traveled more than eighteen hundred miles.[3] And it's not just our food: many of the things we use have traveled vast distances to reach us. Transportation costs are a major factor in making ours the most energy-costly era in history. Ari Fleischer might think of this as the American way of life. But it isn't just American. Increasingly, for those living in affluent parts of our world, it is becoming the modern way, the accepted way, the one we think of as normal.

This modern life we're describing holds many attractions. It's common for people to take vacations in faraway places and to have their own cars, computers, televisions, and fridges. Just a few generations ago, such comforts, if attainable at all, would have been seen as the preserve of the super-rich. Nowadays advertisements give the impression that everyone should have these things, and progress is measured in terms of how much more we have than we used to or how much farther and faster we can go.

One way of thinking about our times is that we are enacting a wonderful success story. Economic and technological development has made many aspects of our lives easier. If we're looking at how to move forward, the path this story suggests is "more of the same, please." We're calling this story Business as Usual.

This is the story told by most mainstream policy makers and corporate leaders. Their view is that economies can, and must, continue to grow. Even in the face of economic downturns and periods of recession, the dominant assumption is that it won't be long before things pick up again. Expressing his trust in the path of economic growth, in November 2010 President Obama said, "The single most important thing we can do to reduce our debt and deficits is to grow."[4]

For a market economy to grow, it needs to increase sales. That means encouraging us to buy, and consume, more than we already do. Advertising plays a key role in stimulating consumption, and increasingly children are targeted as a way of boosting each household's appetite for goods. Estimates suggest that the average American child watches between twenty-five thousand and forty thousand television commercials a year. In the United Kingdom, it is about ten thousand.[5] As we grow up, we learn by watching others. Our views about what's normal and necessary are shaped by what we see.

When you're living in the middle of this story, it's easy to think of it as just the way things are. Young people may be told there is no alternative but to find their place in this scheme of things. Getting ahead is presented as the main plot, supported by the subplots of finding a partner, fending for your family, looking good, and buying stuff. In this view of life, the problems of the world are seen as far away and irrelevant to the dramas of our personal lives.

Transmitted by global media, this story of modern living is catching on around the world and arousing an increasing appetite for consumption. Before 1970 just four items were regarded as essential purchases in China — a bicycle, a sewing machine, a wristwatch, and a radio. By the 1980s a growing consumer class had expanded this list to include a fridge, a color TV, a washing machine, and a tape recorder. A decade later, it had become normal for more and more people in China to have a car, a computer, a mobile phone, and air conditioning.[6] And it's a list that's still growing, as Joe Hatfield, CEO of Walmart Asia, explains:

> We started out with four feet of skin care; today it's twenty feet. Today we don't have deodorants, but someday down the road we will have deodorants in China. Five years ago perfumes were not a big business here. But if you look today it's the emerging market...there's a lot fewer bicycles, so that takes away from the exercise side of it, so people are getting larger, so what's that tell you? Sales of exercise equipment's getting good, exercise wear, jogging outfits, and at some point, we'll have Slimfast and all those type of products.[7]

Some view this as progress.

Box 1.1. Some Core Assumptions of Business as Usual

- Economic growth is essential for prosperity.
- Nature is a commodity to be used for human purposes.
- Promoting consumption is good for the economy.
- The central plot is about getting ahead.
- The problems of other peoples, nations, and species are not our concern.

Why shouldn't people in other parts of the world develop the lifestyle thought of as normal in the West? And why shouldn't we continue with the Business as Usual of economic growth, with people buying more things and using so much energy (see Box 1.1)? To answer those questions, we need to look at the shadow side of modern living and also at where this is taking us. That leads us to our next story.

THE SECOND STORY: THE GREAT UNRAVELING

In 2010 polls for both CBS[8] and Fox News[9] showed that a majority believed the conditions for the next generation would be worse than for people living today. Two years earlier, an international poll of more than 61,600 people in sixty countries yielded similar results.[10] With so many people losing confidence that things will be okay, a very different account of events is emerging. Since it involves a perception that our world is in serious decline, we take a term used by social thinker David Korten and call this story the Great Unraveling.[11]

In our work with people addressing their concerns about the world, we're struck by how many issues are triggering alarm. The list in Box 1.2 identifies five common areas of concern, and most likely you have some others you would add to this list. Facing these problems can feel uncomfortable, even overwhelming, but in order to get to where we want to go, we need to start from where we are. The story of the Great Unraveling offers a disturbing picture of where that is.

Box 1.2. The Great Unraveling of the Early Twenty-First Century

- Economic decline
- Resource depletion
- Climate change
- Social division and war
- Mass extinction of species

Economic Decline

The economic crisis that erupted in 2008 saw not only the collapse of financial institutions but also rising prices, unemployment, home foreclosures, and food riots in many parts of our world. Just a few years earlier, at the beginning of 2005, the global economy was thought of as booming. With house prices rising fast in the United States, property was considered a "safe" investment. There was money to be made in the mortgage business, and loans were freely given, even to those with poor credit ratings. But this boom grew into a bubble that eventually burst. An economist might view this as part of a boom-and-bust cycle. Another phrase we'd use to describe what happened is *overshoot and collapse*. Here's why.

When something moves beyond the point at which it can be sustained, we call this *overshoot*. To restore balance, we need to notice and correct such overextension. If we don't, and the system keeps pushing for more and more, that system can only go so far before reaching a point of breakdown and collapse. The housing market couldn't keep growing indefinitely; neither can the economy.

After years of unsustainable growth, the bubble eventually burst in the US housing market, and in 2006 and 2007 property prices collapsed. Since so many financial institutions were invested in the mortgage industry, the crisis affected the entire economy. Like a row of dominoes, financial giants fell one after the other. Governments borrowed huge amounts of money to prop up ailing institutions that had gone first into overshoot and then into collapse. But what if the whole economic system is in overshoot mode and is now unraveling as a consequence?

The bubble of continuing economic growth depends on an ever-increasing input of resources and generates ever-higher levels of toxic waste. The more we push beyond sustainable limits for both of these, the more the unraveling occurs.

Resource Depletion

In 1859, when the first of the US oil fields was discovered in Pennsylvania, the world's population stood at just over a billion people. By 1930 it had doubled, and by 1974, with increased food production from oil-powered agriculture, it doubled again to 4 billion. We are already well on the way to another doubling, with global population passing the 7 billion mark in 2011. It isn't just population that's growing; the spread of modern lifestyles, as discussed above, has amplified our appetites, especially for energy.

In the twentieth century, global consumption of fossil fuels increased twentyfold. Oil has been our dominant fuel, and we are now consuming more than 80 million barrels a day. If we continue at this rate, we will use up available supplies within a few decades.[12] Problems start long before we run out; as oil fields become depleted, the remaining reserves become more difficult and costly to extract. The same is true of the world's supply as a whole. As a result, fuel prices are rising and the age of cheap oil is already behind us.

Each big rise in the price of oil over the last thirty-five years has been followed by a recession, with the price of oil doubling in just twelve months prior to the economic downturn of 2008.[13] When oil production levels move past their peak and into decline (the point referred to as "peak oil"), the inability to meet demand will push prices through the roof.

We're unlikely to be rescued by new oil source discoveries; for the last three decades more oil has been consumed each year than has been found in new reserves. By 2006 that deficit had grown to four barrels used up for every new barrel discovered.[14] What's more, the new reserves are either difficult to reach, as is the case with the deep-water wells over a mile beneath the ocean's surface, or are of much poorer quality, as is the case with the tar sands in Canada.

Our collective oil consumption cannot be sustained. If we don't address this issue, we will be heading for a crash.

Even more crucial to life on our planet, the availability of freshwater is also in decline. A recent United Nations report warns that within twenty years, as much as two-thirds of the world's population could be at risk of water shortages.[15] Industrialization, irrigation, population growth, and modern lifestyles have dramatically increased our water consumption, with water use increasing sixfold during the twentieth century.[16] Climate change has also been a factor, with more rain in some parts of the world but much less in others. Since 1970 severe droughts have increased, and the proportion of the Earth's land surface suffering very dry conditions has grown from 15 to 30 percent.[17]

Climate Change

When more people consume more things, we not only deplete resources, but we also produce more waste. The rubbish generated each year in the United States could fill a convoy of garbage trucks long enough to go round the world six times.[18] Not all our waste is so visible: each year, the average European puts out 8.1 tons of carbon dioxide; the average American more than double this.[19] While this greenhouse gas is invisible, its effects are not. Climate change is no longer only a distant threat for future generations: it has arrived in measurable and destructive form.

At the time, the 1980s was the warmest decade ever recorded. The 1990s were even warmer, and the decade starting in 2000 warmer still.[20] Linked to this warming, weather-related disasters (including floods, droughts, and major hurricanes) have increased dramatically: on average, three hundred events were recorded every year in the 1980s, 480 events every year in the 1990s, and 620 events every year in the decade up to 2008. In 2007 there were 874 weather-related disasters worldwide.[21]

As warming causes water to evaporate more quickly, land is drying out so much in some parts of the world that crops are failing and wildfires are becoming more intense. In Brazil, the droughts in 2005 were considered a once-a-century event. Yet the droughts that followed in 2010 were even worse. In Washington State, there has been more forest loss from wildfires in the last ten years than in the previous three decades combined.[22]

At the same time, warmer winds carry more water from the oceans, causing other areas to suffer an increase in flooding and extreme rainfall events. Ronald Neilson, a professor of bioclimatology at Oregon State University, explains: "As the planet warms, more water is getting evaporated from the oceans and all that water has to come down somewhere as precipitation."[23]

In Bangladesh, fourteen inches of rain fell in a single day in 2004, contributing to floods that left 10 million homeless and much of the crop yield destroyed. The floods in Pakistan in 2010 put a fifth of the country underwater, displacing 20 million people.

Most of the world's major cities developed as ports bordering the sea or major rivers, and more than 630 million people live less than thirty-three feet above sea level. If the ice sheets in Greenland and West Antarctica continue melting, rising water levels will flood London, New York, Miami, Mumbai, Calcutta, Sydney, Shanghai, Jakarta, Tokyo, and many other major cities.[24] Melting ice is also significant because land and sea surfaces absorb more of the sun's warmth than ice cover does. This creates a vicious cycle (see Box 1.3), in which the more the ice melts, the less it reflects the sun's heat and the warmer it gets, leading to further ice melting.

Forests play a protective role by absorbing carbon dioxide, but as woodlands are chopped down, we lose this crucial process. Tropical trees are additionally at risk because when warmer air dries out the soil beyond a certain point, the ground can no longer support large trees. A global temperature increase of 7.2°F (4°C) could be enough to kill much of the Amazon rain forest.[25] If this happened, not only would we lose the forest's cooling effect, but the greenhouse gases released from rotting or burning trees would further add to warming, setting off another vicious cycle. The term *runaway climate change* is used to describe this dangerous situation, in which the consequences of warming cause more warming to occur (see Box 1.3). Professor Kevin Anderson of the Tyndall Centre for Climate Change warns of the catastrophe this could lead to:

> For humanity, it's a matter of life or death...it's extremely unlikely that we wouldn't have mass death at 4°C. If you have got a population of nine billion by 2050 and you hit 4°C, 5°C or 6°C, you might have half a billion people surviving.[26]

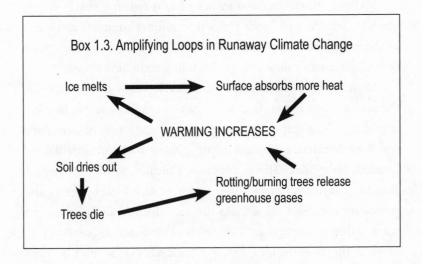

Box 1.3. Amplifying Loops in Runaway Climate Change

Ice melts ⟶ Surface absorbs more heat

WARMING INCREASES

Soil dries out

Trees die ⟶ Rotting/burning trees release greenhouse gases

Social Division and War

At the moment, the poor of our world are bearing the brunt of the Great Unraveling. As oil prices have gone up, the cost of food has rocketed. Global food prices more than doubled between February 2001 and February 2011, pushing more and more people below the poverty line.[27] In 2010 more than 900 million people suffered chronic hunger. Meanwhile, the richest 20 percent of our world's population (that's anyone able to spend more than $10 a day) receive three-quarters of the total income.[28]

. While some argue that economic growth is needed to tackle poverty, wealth has flowed much more to the rich than to the poor as the global economy has grown. The number of millionaires and billionaires increases, while nearly half the world's population still lives on less than $2.50 a day.[29] Within affluent countries too, the gap between rich and poor has grown wider. Twenty-five years ago, the richest 1 percent in the United States earned 12 percent of the national income and owned 33 percent of the wealth. In 2011 they earned nearly a quarter of the income and owned 40 percent of the wealth.[30] Studies show the more economically divided a society becomes, the more trust levels fall, crime increases, and communities fall apart.[31]

The UN Millennium Project estimates that extreme poverty and world hunger could be eliminated by 2025 for a cost of approximately $160 billion a year.[32] The world's military spending in 2010 was ten times that amount, with the US government spending almost as much as all the other countries in the world put together.[33] The unraveling of our world comes, in part, from seeking security through battling enemies rather than addressing the threats presented by deepening inequalities, resource depletion, and climate change.

Mass Extinction of Species

With rising pollution, habitat destruction, and the disturbance wrought by climate change, the toll on wildlife has been enormous. A third of all amphibians, at least a fifth of all mammals, and an eighth of all bird species are now threatened with extinction. "The Global Biodiversity Outlook," a UN report, concluded:

In effect, we are currently responsible for the sixth major extinction event in the history of Earth, and the greatest since the dinosaurs disappeared, 65 million years ago.[34]

Some species play critical roles in the healthy functioning of natural systems; we depend on them for our survival. Microscopic plankton in the oceans, for example, is the food that fish depend on; these plankton also produce much of the oxygen we breathe. When carbon dioxide from burning fossil fuels is absorbed by the oceans, it makes the seawater more acidic, harming the plankton. The combination of ocean acidity and warming water has already led to a dramatic decline in the global population of plankton.[35] If this decline continues, we don't know at what point it will yield catastrophic consequences — such as the collapse of fish life or a substantial reduction in the oxygen available to us.

THE DOUBLE REALITY

The stories of Business as Usual and the Great Unraveling offer starkly contrasting accounts of the state of our world. They are two different realities coexisting in the same time and space. You probably know people who live in a different story than you. You may also be moving between stories yourself. It's possible to spend part of a day in our own business-as-usual mode, making plans for a future we assume will be much like today. Then something triggers an awareness of the mess we're in, and we recognize in our hearts and minds the crash that lies ahead.

For increasing numbers of people, the crash has come already: homes flooded after extreme rainfall, farms abandoned because of long-term drought, water supplies contaminated and undrinkable, jobs or savings lost. The mainstream reality of Business as Usual is increasingly becoming interrupted by the bad news of the Great Unraveling.

When we first become aware of the grimness of our situation, it can come as quite a shock. Most of these issues are squeezed out of mainstream media, their coverage confined to occasional documentaries or fringe publications. The gaze of the modern press, particularly in the Western world, is more focused on gossip about celebrities. We live, as Al Gore puts it, in a culture of distraction.[36]

When these issues do come up in conversation, they are often met by awkward silences. Two different views commonly block the flow of words. The first dismisses the problem as overblown. This is the voice of the first story that says it's not really that bad. The second perspective fully inhabits the Great Unraveling. This view sees continued decline as so inevitable as to render it not worth talking about. There is a resigned acceptance that things have gone too far, that we can't do anything about them, that we've crossed a point of no return.

The expression *things have gone too far* is another way of saying we are in overshoot. We are too late to prevent the harm already done or to prevent aspects of collapse already well under way. Overfishing has already led to the devastating collapse of many of the world's fisheries. Climate change has already led to an increase in extreme weather events worldwide. Many oil-producing countries (including the United States, the United Kingdom, and Russia) are already past their production peak, their oil output now in decline.[37] These things have already happened. But we can learn from them and make choices about where we go from here. In their detailed study of the global overshoot in our material economy, environmental scientists Donnella Meadows, Jørgen Randers, and Dennis Meadows write:

> Overshoot can lead to two different outcomes. One is a crash of some kind. Another is a deliberate turnaround, a correction, a careful easing down.... We believe that a correction is possible and that it could lead to a desirable, sustainable,

sufficient future for all the world's peoples. We also believe that if a profound correction is not made soon, a crash of some sort is certain. And it will occur within the lifetimes of many who are alive today.[38]

The story of Business as Usual is putting us on a collision course with disaster. And by itself, the Great Unraveling can seem like a horror story that overwhelms and defeats, paralyzing us. Fortunately there is a third story, one that is becoming increasingly visible. You are probably already part of it.

THE THIRD STORY: THE GREAT TURNING

In the Agricultural Revolution of ten thousand years ago, the domestication of plants and animals led to a radical shift in the way people lived. In the Industrial Revolution that began just a few hundred years ago, a similar dramatic transition took place. These weren't just changes in the small details of people's lives. The whole basis of society was transformed, including people's relationship with one another and with Earth.

Right now a shift of comparable scope and magnitude is occurring. It's been called the Ecological Revolution, the Sustainability Revolution, even the Necessary Revolution. This is our third story: we call it the Great Turning and see it as the essential adventure of our time. It involves the transition from a doomed economy of industrial growth to a life-sustaining society committed to the recovery of our world. This transition is already well under way.

In the early stages of major transitions, the initial activity might seem to exist only at the fringes. Yet when their time comes, ideas and behaviors become contagious: the more people pass on inspiring perspectives, the more these perspectives catch on. At a certain point, the balance tips and we reach critical mass. Viewpoints and practices that were once on the margins become the new mainstream.

In the story of the Great Turning, what's catching on is commitment to act for the sake of life on Earth as well as the vision, courage, and solidarity to do so. Social and technical innovations converge, mobilizing people's energy, attention, creativity, and determination, in what Paul Hawken describes as "the largest social movement in history." In his book *Blessed Unrest*, he writes, "I soon realized that my initial estimate of 100,000 organizations was off by at least a factor of ten, and I now believe there are over one — and maybe even two — million organizations working towards ecological sustainability and social justice."[39]

Don't be surprised if you haven't read about this epic transition in major newspapers or seen it reported in other mainstream media. Their focus is usually trained on sudden, discrete events they can point their cameras at. Cultural shifts happen on a different level; they come into view only when we step back enough to see a bigger picture changing over time. A newspaper photograph viewed through a magnifying glass may appear only as tiny dots. When it seems as if our lives and choices are like those dots, it can be difficult to recognize their contribution to a bigger picture of change. We might need to train ourselves to see the larger pattern and recognize how the story of the Great Turning is happening in our time. Once seen, it becomes easier to recognize. And when we name it, this story becomes more real and familiar to us.

As an aid to appreciating the ways you may already be part of this story, we identify three dimensions of the Great Turning. They are mutually reinforcing and equally necessary. For convenience, we've labeled them as first, second, and third dimensions, but that is not to suggest any order of sequence or importance. We can start at any point, and beginning at one naturally leads into either of the others. It is for each of us to follow our own sense of rightness about where we feel called to act.

The First Dimension: Holding Actions

Holding actions aim to hold back and slow down the damage being caused by the political economy of Business as Usual. The goal is to protect what is left of our natural life-support systems, rescuing what we can of our biodiversity, clean air and water, forests, and topsoil. Holding actions also counter the unraveling of our social fabric, caring for those who have been damaged and safeguarding communities against exploitation, war, starvation, and injustice. Holding actions defend our shared existence and the integrity of life on this, our planet home.

This dimension includes raising awareness of the damage being done, gathering evidence of and documenting the environmental, social, and health impacts of industrial growth. We need the work of scientists, campaigners, and journalists, revealing the links between pollution and rising childhood cancers; fossil fuel consumption and climate disturbance; the availability of cheap products and sweatshop working conditions. Unless these connections are clearly made, it is too easy to go on unconsciously contributing to the unraveling of our world. We become part of the story of the Great Turning when we increase our awareness, seek to learn more, and alert others to the issues we all face.

There are many ways we can act. We can choose to remove our support for behaviors and products we know to be part of the problem. Joining with others, we can add to the strength of campaigns, petitions, boycotts, rallies, legal proceedings, direct actions, and other forms of protest against practices that threaten our world. While holding actions can be frustrating when met with slow progress or defeat, they have also led to important victories. Areas of old-growth forests in Canada, the United States, Poland, and Australia, for example, have been protected through determined and sustained activism.

Holding actions are essential; they save lives, they save species and ecosystems, they save some of the gene pool for future generations. But by themselves, they are not enough for the Great Turning to occur. For every acre of forest protected, many others are lost to logging or clearance. For every species brought back from the brink, others are lost to extinction. Vital as protest is, relying on it as a sole avenue of change can leave us battle-weary or disillusioned. Along with stopping the damage, we need to replace or transform the systems that cause the harm. This is the work of the second dimension.

The Second Dimension: Life-Sustaining Systems and Practices

If you look for it, you can find evidence that our civilization is being reinvented all around us. Previously accepted approaches to health-care, business, education, agriculture, transportation, communication, psychology, economics, and so many other areas are being questioned and transformed. This is the second strand of the Great Turning, and it involves a rethinking of the way we do things, as well as a creative redesign of the structures and systems that make up our society.

The financial crisis in 2008 caused many to start questioning our banking system. In a poll that year, over half those interviewed said interest rates used to be their main concern, but now they also considered other factors, such as where the money was invested and what it was doing.[40] Alongside this shift in thinking, new types of banks, like Triodos Bank, are rewriting the rules of finance by operating on the model of "triple return." In this model investments bring not only financial return but also social and environmental benefits. The more people put their savings into this kind of investment, the more funds become available for enterprises that aim for greater benefits than just making money. This in turn fuels the development of a new economic sector based on the triple bottom line. These investments have proved to be remarkably stable at a time of economic turbulence, putting ethical banks in a strong financial position.

One area benefiting from such investment is the agricultural sector, which has seen a swing to environmentally and socially responsible practices. Concerned about the toxic effects of pesticides and other chemicals used in industrial farming, large numbers of people have switched to buying and eating organic produce. Fair-trade initiatives improve the working conditions of producers, while community supported agriculture (CSA) and farmers' markets cut food miles by increasing the availability of local produce. In these and other areas, strong, green shoots are sprouting, as new organizational systems grow out of the visionary question, "Is there a better way to do things — one that brings benefits rather than causing harm?" In some areas, like green building, design principles that were considered on the fringe a few years ago are now finding widespread acceptance.

When we support and participate in these emerging strands of a life-sustaining culture, we become part of the Great Turning. Through our choices about how to travel, where to shop, what to buy, and how to save, we shape the development of this new economy. Social enterprises, micro-energy projects, community teach-ins, sustainable agriculture, and ethical financial systems all contribute to the rich patchwork quilt of a life-sustaining society. By themselves, however, they are not enough. These new structures won't take root and survive without deeply ingrained values to sustain them. This is the work of the third dimension of the Great Turning.

The Third Dimension: Shift in Consciousness

What inspires people to embark on projects or support campaigns that are not of immediate personal benefit? At the core of our consciousness is a wellspring of caring and compassion; this aspect of ourselves — which we might think of as our *connected self* — can be nurtured and developed. We can deepen our sense of belonging in the world. Like trees extending their root system, we can grow in connection, thus allowing ourselves to draw from a deeper pool of strength, accessing the courage and intelligence we so greatly need right now. This dimension of the Great Turning arises from shifts taking place in our hearts, our minds, and our views of reality. It involves insights and practices that resonate with venerable spiritual traditions, while in alignment with revolutionary new understandings from science.

A significant event in this part of the story is the *Apollo 8* spaceflight of December 1968. Because of this mission to the moon, and the photos it produced, humanity had its first sighting of Earth as a whole. Twenty years earlier, the astronomer Sir Fred Hoyle had said, "Once a photograph of the Earth taken from the outside is available, a new idea as powerful as any in history will be let loose."[41] Bill Anders, the astronaut who took those first photos, commented, "We came all this way to explore the moon and the most important thing is that we discovered the Earth."[42]

We are among the first in human history to have had this remarkable view. It came at the same time as the development in science of a radical new understanding of how our world works. Looking at our planet as a whole, Gaia theory proposes that the Earth functions as a self-regulating living system.

During the past forty years, those Earth photos, along with Gaia theory and environmental challenges, have provoked the emergence of a new way of thinking about ourselves. No longer just citizens of this country or that, we are discovering a deeper collective identity. As many indigenous traditions have taught for generations, we are part of the Earth.

A shift in consciousness is taking place, as we move into a larger landscape of what we are. With this evolutionary jump comes a beautiful convergence of two areas previously thought to clash: science and spirituality. The awareness of a deeper unity connecting us lies at the heart of many spiritual traditions; insights from modern science point in a similar direction. We live at a time when a new view of reality is emerging, where spiritual insight and scientific discovery both contribute to our understanding of ourselves as intimately interwoven with our world.

We take part in this third dimension of the Great Turning when we pay attention to the inner frontier of change, to the personal and spiritual development that enhances our capacity and desire to act for our world. By strengthening our compassion, we give fuel to our courage and determination. By refreshing our sense of belonging in the world, we widen the web of relationships that nourishes us and protects us from burnout. In the past, changing the self and changing the world were often regarded as separate endeavors and viewed in either-or terms. But in the story of the Great Turning, they are recognized as mutually reinforcing and essential to one another (see Box 1.4).

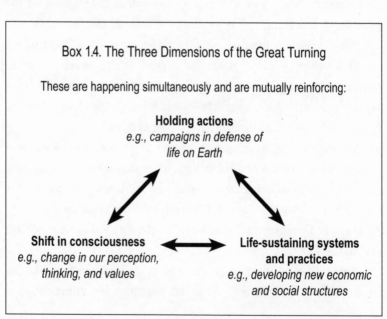

Box 1.4. The Three Dimensions of the Great Turning

These are happening simultaneously and are mutually reinforcing:

Holding actions
*e.g., campaigns in defense of
life on Earth*

Shift in consciousness
*e.g., change in our perception,
thinking, and values*

**Life-sustaining systems
and practices**
*e.g., developing new economic
and social structures*

ACTIVE HOPE AND THE STORY OF OUR LIVES

Future generations will look back at the time we are living in now. The kind of future they look from, and the story they tell about our period, will be shaped by choices we make in our lifetimes. The most telling choice of all may well be the story we live from and see ourselves participating in. It sets the context of our lives in a way that influences all our other decisions.

In choosing our story, we not only cast our vote of influence over the kind of world future generations inherit, but we also affect our own lives in the here and now. When we find a good story and fully give ourselves to it, that story can act through us, breathing new life into everything we do. When we move in a direction that touches our heart, we add to the momentum of deeper purpose that makes us feel more alive. A great story and a satisfying life share a vital element: a compelling plot that moves toward meaningful goals, where what is at stake is far larger than our personal gains and losses. The Great Turning is such a story.

CHAPTER TWO

Trusting the Spiral

Active Hope is not wishful thinking.
Active Hope is not waiting to be rescued
by the Lone Ranger or by some savior.
Active Hope is waking up to the beauty of life
on whose behalf we can act.
We belong to this world.
The web of life is calling us forth at this time.
We've come a long way and are here to play our part.
With Active Hope we realize that there are adventures in store,
strengths to discover, and comrades to link arms with.
Active Hope is a readiness to engage.
Active Hope is a readiness to discover the strengths
in ourselves and in others;
a readiness to discover the reasons for hope
and the occasions for love.
A readiness to discover the size and strength of our hearts,
our quickness of mind, our steadiness of purpose,
our own authority, our love for life,
the liveliness of our curiosity,
the unsuspected deep well of patience and diligence,
the keenness of our senses, and our capacity to lead.
None of these can be discovered in an armchair or without risk.

The Great Turning is a story of Active Hope. To play our best part, we need to counter the voices that say we're not up to the task, that we're not good enough, strong enough, or wise enough to make any difference. If we fear that the mess we're in is too awful to look at or that we won't be able to cope with the distress it brings up, we need to find a way through that fear. This chapter describes three threads we can follow that help us stand tall and not shrink away when facing the immensity of what's happening to our world. These threads can be woven into any situation as a way of supporting and strengthening our capacity to respond. We shall therefore return to them often in the pages ahead. The first thread is the narrative structure of adventure stories.

FOLLOWING THE THREAD OF ADVENTURE

Think of the Great Turning as an adventure story. Adventure stories often begin by introducing an ominous threat that seems way beyond what the main characters are capable of dealing with. If you ever feel the odds are stacked against you and doubt whether you're up to the challenge, then you join a time-honored tradition of protagonists in this genre. Heroes almost always start out seeming distinctly underpowered.

What makes the story is the way the central characters are not put off. Instead, their tale sets them on a quest in search of the allies, tools, and wisdom needed to improve their chances. We can think of ourselves as on a similar journey; part of the adventure of the Great Turning involves seeking the company, sources of support, tools, and insights that help us.

What starts us off is seeing what's at stake and feeling called to play our part. Then we just follow the thread of the adventure, developing capacities along the way and discovering hidden strengths that only reveal themselves when needed. When things are bumpy or bleak, we can remind ourselves that this is how these stories often go. There may be times when all feels lost. That too can be part of the story. Our choices at such moments can make a crucial difference.

THE THREAD OF ACTIVE HOPE

Any situation we face can resolve in a range of different ways — some much better, others much worse. Active Hope involves identifying the outcomes we hope for and then playing an active role in bringing them about. We don't wait until we are sure of success. We don't limit our choices to the outcomes that seem likely. Instead, we focus on what we truly, deeply long for, and then we proceed to take determined steps in that direction. This is the second thread we follow.

We can react to world crises in many different ways, with a spectrum of possible responses, from our best to our worst. We can rise to the occasion with wisdom, courage, and care, or we can shrink from the challenge, blot it out, or look away. With Active Hope we consciously choose to draw out our best responses, so that we might surprise even ourselves by what we bring forth. Can we train ourselves to become more courageous, inspired, and connected? This takes us to the next thread.

THE THREAD OF THE SPIRAL OF THE WORK THAT RECONNECTS

The spiral of the Work That Reconnects is something we can come back to again and again as a source of strength and fresh insights. It reminds us that we are larger, stronger, deeper, and more creative than we have been brought up to believe. It maps out an empowerment process that journeys through four successive movements, or stations, described as Coming from Gratitude, Honoring Our Pain for the World, Seeing with New Eyes, and Going Forth.

When we come from gratitude, we become more present to the wonder of being alive in this amazing living world, to the many gifts we receive, to the beauty we appreciate. Yet the very act of looking at what we love and value in our world brings with it an awareness of the vast violation under way, the despoliation and unraveling. From gratitude we naturally flow to honoring our pain for the world.

Coming from gratitude helps build a context of trust and psychological buoyancy that supports us to face difficult realities in the second phase. Dedicating time and attention to honoring our pain for the world ensures that there is space to hear our sorrow, grief, outrage, and any other feelings revealing themselves in response to what is happening to our world. Admitting the depths of our anguish, even to ourselves, takes us into culturally forbidden territory. From an early age we've been told to pull ourselves together, to cheer up or shut up. By honoring our pain for the world, we break through the taboos that silence our distress. When the activating siren of inner alarm is no longer muffled or shut out, something gets switched on inside us. It is our survival response.

The term *honoring* implies a respectful welcoming, where we recognize the value of something. Our pain for the world not only alerts us to danger but also reveals our profound caring. And this caring derives from our interconnectedness with all life. We need not fear it.

In the third stage, we step further into the perceptual shift that recognizes our pain for the world as a healthy expression of our belonging to life. Seeing with new eyes reveals the wider web of resources available to us through our rootedness within a deeper, ecological self. This third stage draws on insights from holistic science and ancient spiritual wisdom, as well as from our creative imaginations. It opens us to a new view of what is possible and a new understanding of our power to make a difference.

To experience the benefits of these empowering perspectives, we want to apply them to the task of addressing the challenges we face. The final station, Going Forth, involves clarifying our vision of how we can act for the healing of our world, identifying practical steps that move our vision forward (see Fig. 2).

Figure 2. The spiral of the Work That Reconnects

The spiral offers a transformational journey that deepens our capacity to act for the sake of life on Earth. We call it a spiral rather than a cycle because every time we move through the four stations we experience them differently. Each element reconnects us with our world, and each encounter can surprise us with hidden gems. As each station naturally unfolds into the next, a momentum and a flow build up, allowing the four elements to work together to form a whole that is more than the sum of its parts. As we allow ourselves to be guided by this spiral form, it isn't just us acting; we are letting the world act on us and through us.

THE WORK THAT RECONNECTS AS A PERSONAL PRACTICE

The spiral provides a structure we can fall back on, and into, whenever we need to tap into the resilience and resourcefulness arising from the larger web of life. If you're feeling sickened by a disturbing news report, you can step into gratitude simply by focusing on your breath and taking a moment to give thanks for whatever may be sustaining you in that moment. As you feel the air entering your nostrils, give thanks for oxygen, for your lungs, for all that brings you to life. The question, "To whom am I grateful?" moves your attention beyond yourself to those you receive from, those who support you.

A moment of gratitude strengthens your capacity to look at, rather than turn away from, disturbing information. As you allow yourself to take in whatever you see, allow yourself also to feel whatever you feel. When you experience pain for something beyond your immediate self-interest, this reveals your caring, compassion, and connection — such precious things. By honoring your pain for the world, in whatever form it takes, you take it seriously and allow the signal it brings to rouse you.

When seeing with new eyes, you know that it isn't just you facing this. You are just one part of a much larger story, a continuing stream of life on Earth that has flowed for more than three and a half billion years and that has survived five mass extinctions. When you sink into this deeper, stronger flow and experience yourself as part of it, a different set of possibilities emerges. Widening your vision increases the resources available to you, since through the same channels of connectedness that pain for the world flows, so also do strength, courage, renewed determination, and the help of allies.

With the shift of perception that seeing with new eyes brings, you can let go of feeling you need to sort everything out. Instead you focus on finding and playing your part, offering your gift of Active Hope, your best contribution to the healing of our world. As you move into going forth, you consider what this might be, and what your next step will be. Then you take that step.

What we've described here is a short form of the spiral that might only take a few minutes to move round. Like a fractal that has the same characteristic shape whatever scale it is viewed at, the form of the spiral can be applied to a wide range of time frames, with rotations happening over minutes, hours, days, or weeks. We move through the four stations in a way that supports our intention to act for the sake of life on Earth. The more familiar you become with this strengthening journey, the more you can trust the spiral structure process. Each of these stations contains hidden depths, rich meaning, and treasures to explore. It is to these that we turn in the chapters ahead.

CHAPTER THREE

Coming from Gratitude

"A felt sense of wonder, thankfulness, and appreciation for life" is how the renowned psychologist Robert Emmons defines gratitude.[1] If you're feeling low, it might seem like a stretch to focus on something so positive. Yet recognizing the gifts in your life is profoundly strengthening. By savoring these gifts, you add to your psychological buoyancy, which helps you maintain your balance and poise when entering rougher waters. That is why we begin our workshops this way. Gratitude enhances our resilience, strengthening us to face disturbing information.

GRATITUDE PROMOTES A SENSE OF WELL-BEING

Recent research has shown that people experiencing high levels of gratitude tend to be happier and more satisfied with their lives.[2] Are they grateful *because* they're happy, or does gratitude *make* people happier? To find out, volunteers were asked to keep gratitude journals, in which, at regular intervals, they recorded events they felt thankful for. Controlled trials have shown this simple intervention to have a profound and reliable impact on mood.[3] Indeed, the results are so striking that if a medication were invented with similar benefits, we'd probably see it described as a new wonder drug.

The process of keeping a gratitude journal focuses your attention on things you feel good about. If each evening, before you go to bed, you ask yourself, "What happened today that I'm pleased about or thankful for?" that question will direct your gaze. You start searching your memory for moments that bring a smile to your face or that trigger a glow of appreciation. They might be small things, such as a conversation with a friend, a moment watching a bird in flight, or the satisfaction of completing a task. When we're busy, moments like these can too easily pass us by. Keeping a gratitude diary builds them into a pool of memories we can keep dipping back into.

When we get into the habit of keeping this kind of journal, we train our minds to notice the upside of life more easily and quickly. Experiencing gratitude is a learnable skill that improves with practice. It isn't dependent on things going well or on receiving favors from others. It's about getting better at spotting what's already there.

TRY THIS: A GRATITUDE PRACTICE

Notice: Scan your recent memories and identify something that's happened in the last twenty-four hours that you're pleased about. It doesn't have to be anything big, just something that makes you think, "I'm glad that happened."

Savor: Close your eyes and imagine that you are experiencing that moment again. Notice colors, tastes, sounds, smells, and the sensations in your body. Notice also how you feel in yourself.

Give thanks: Who or what helped this moment to happen? Was anyone (or anything) else involved? If so, think of them and imagine expressing your thanks.

There are two sides to gratitude: the first is appreciation, where you're valuing something that has happened, and the second is attribution, where you're recognizing the role of someone or something else in bringing it about. Even when you're grateful to yourself, it is likely that others played a role in your development of the skill, strength, or quality you used. Gratitude is a social emotion. It points our warmth and goodwill out toward others.

GRATITUDE BUILDS TRUST AND GENEROSITY

Think of the people you trust. Do you also feel grateful toward them or suspect they feel gratitude toward you? Gratitude feeds trust, because it helps us acknowledge the times we've been able to count on one another. Not surprisingly, research shows we're more likely to help those we feel grateful to, leading to a positive spiral of helping, gratitude, trust, and cooperation.[4] Because of this, gratitude plays a key role in the evolution of cooperative behavior and societies.

When gratitude levels are high, not only are we more inclined to return favors, but we're also more likely to assist complete strangers. In the 1970s American psychologist Alice Isen demonstrated this in an experiment in which coins were left in public phone booths so that the next person using them would get a free call.[5] When the person had finished and was leaving the phone booth, one of the experimenters appeared to accidentally drop a file of papers just in front of the subject. This process was repeated near phone boxes that hadn't been primed with coins. People receiving the unexpected lucky gift of a free phone call were much more likely to help the experimenter pick up her papers. This experiment, and a host of others like it, suggests that our willingness to act on behalf of others isn't just attributable to some people being good-natured and others less so. Our readiness to help others is influenced by the level of gratitude we experience.

GRATITUDE AS AN ANTIDOTE TO CONSUMERISM

While gratitude leads to increased happiness and life satisfaction, materialism — placing a higher value on material possessions than on meaningful relationships — has the opposite effect. In reviewing the research, psychologists Emily Polak and Michael McCullough conclude: "The pursuit of wealth and possessions as an end unto itself is associated with lower levels of well-being, lower life satisfaction and happiness, more symptoms of depression and anxiety, more physical problems such as headaches, and a variety of mental disorders."[6]

Affluenza is a term used to describe the emotional distress that arises from a preoccupation with possessions and appearance. Psychologist Oliver James views it as a form of psychological virus that infects our thinking and is transmitted by television, glossy magazines, and advertisements. The toxic belief at the core of this condition is that happiness is based on how we look and what we have. If we compare our appearance or wealth to that of the models and millionaires on prime-time television, it is easy to feel we don't measure up so well. James comments, "Since programmes are saturated with exceptionally attractive people living abnormally opulent lives, expectations of what is 'normal' are raised."[7]

When women were asked to rate their self-esteem and satisfaction with their appearance, measures for both fell after the women looked at photos of models in women's magazines.[8] How we feel depends so much on what we compare ourselves to, and an increase in eating disorders is one of the consequences of having thin models as a reference group. In 1995, the year television was introduced to Fiji, there were no recorded cases of bulimia on the island. Yet within three years, 11 percent of young Fijian women were found to be suffering from this eating disorder.[9]

Gratitude is about delighting in and feeling satisfied with what you're already experiencing. The advertising industry aims to undermine this by convincing you that you're missing something. On a website for marketing professionals, the advertiser's Law of Dissatisfaction is described like this:

> The job of advertisers is to create dissatisfaction in its audience. If people are happy with how they look, they are not going to buy cosmetics or diet books....If people are happy with who they are, where they are in life, and what they got, they just aren't customer potential — that is, unless you make them unhappy.
>
> Most cosmetic advertisements feature beautiful women, igniting the promise that you too can look like a drop-dead glorious model if only you use the product. This approach is based on showing an ideal that the audience will undoubtedly be unable to stack up against. The audience, after seeing what they could look like, is no longer happy with what they do look like, and they are now motivated to buy into the promise of change.[10]

Each year, more than four hundred billion dollars are spent on advertising that pushes the message "buy this, and your life will improve." Yet even though people in materially rich countries buy many more things than they did fifty years ago, surveys show they are less happy (see Box 3.1).[11] Depression has reached epidemic proportions, with one in two people in the Western world likely to suffer a significant episode at some point in their lives.[12] The consumer lifestyle isn't just wrecking our world; it is also making us miserable. Can gratitude play a role in our rehabilitation?

Box 3.1. Ponder Point

More resources have been consumed in the last fifty years than in all preceding human history.[13] Yet we're not any happier, and depression has reached epidemic proportions.

In looking at what drives materialism, researcher Tim Kasser identifies two main factors: feelings of insecurity and exposure to social models expressing materialistic values.[14] Gratitude, by promoting feelings of trust, helps counter insecurity. By making us more likely to return favors and help others, it also encourages us to act in ways that strengthen the networks of support around us. As Polak and McCullough point out, "Gratitude alerts us that there are people out there with our well-being in mind and it motivates us to deepen our own reservoirs of social capital through reciprocation."[15]

Gratitude and materialism offer different stories about what we need in order to feel secure. With materialism, security is based on having the right things: we know what these right things are by keeping an eye on our neighbors and on current fashions. Insecurity grows when we feel we're falling behind, and pressure builds to "keep up with the Joneses" in a way that further drives consumption.

Gratitude pulls us out of this rat race. It shifts our focus from what's missing to what's there. If we were to design a cultural therapy that protected us from depression and, at the same time, helped reduce consumerism, it would surely include cultivating our ability to experience gratitude. Training ourselves in the skill of gratitude is part of the Great Turning.

TRY THIS: OPEN SENTENCES ON GRATITUDE

Read the following beginnings of sentences, and see what words seem to naturally follow. You can think this to yourself, or put it in writing, or try it with a partner, taking turns to speak and listen. It is worth devoting a few minutes or more to each sentence. Whenever you're not sure what to say, come back to the beginning of the sentence and see what naturally follows — it may be different each time you do this.

Some things I love about being alive on Earth are...
A place that was magical to me as a child was...
My favorite activities include...
Someone who helped me believe in myself is or was...
Some things I appreciate about myself are...

BLOCKS TO GRATITUDE

At times gratitude comes easily. If you're falling in love, having a run of good luck, or just generally delighted with how things are going, appreciation and thankfulness might feel natural. But what if there isn't so much to feel happy about? What about the times when relationships go sour, you experience injury or violation, or the landscape of your life looks bleak?

If you're facing a tragedy in your life or in the world, searching for reasons to be grateful might initially feel uncomfortably close to denial. But you don't have to feel thankful for everything that's happened. It is more a case of recognizing there's always a larger picture, a bigger view, and that it contains both positive and negative aspects. To find our power to see the hard parts clearly and respond constructively, we need to draw on resources that bring out the best in us. Gratitude does this. It's a resource we can learn to tap into at any moment. Here's an example.

Julia had just seen the news. She felt outraged. A school in a refugee camp had been bombed, children killed, she was so full of fury she could hardly speak about anything else. Then, for a moment, she thought of the reporters who covered this story. They had risked their lives so that she could be kept informed. The news editors may also have stuck their necks out, choosing to include this item rather than the latest celebrity gossip. As she thought

*about the steps they had taken, she felt grateful. Her gratitude
reminded her she wasn't alone in caring about what happened.*

When violations and injustice occur, trust is often a casualty.
Loss of trust makes it harder to experience gratitude; even when
help is given, the distrustful part of us may wonder what the hidden
agendas are. Trust levels are falling; surveys show that people are
about half as likely to trust others as they were fifty years ago.[16] Will
it be possible to turn the tide? Trust and gratitude feed each other:
to deepen our capacity for thankfulness in difficult times, we need to
learn from those who have mastered this quality.

LEARNING FROM THE HAUDENOSAUNEE

In autumn 1977, delegates from the Haudenosaunee, Native Americans also known as the Iroquois Confederacy, traveled to a UN
conference in Geneva, Switzerland. They had a warning and a
prophecy to share, presenting it alongside a description of their core
values and view of the world. Their "Basic Call to Consciousness,"
as it is known, contained the following paragraph:

> The original instructions direct that we who walk about on
> the Earth are to express a great respect, an affection, and a
> gratitude toward all the spirits which create and support Life.
> We give a greeting and thanksgiving to the many supporters
> of our own lives — the corn, beans, squash, the winds, the
> sun. When people cease to respect and express gratitude for
> these many things, then all life will be destroyed, and human
> life on this planet will come to an end.

The Haudenosaunee regard gratitude as essential to survival.
From the perspective of Western individualism, that view might
seem hard to grasp. In the Business as Usual story, self-made success

is among the most highly prized of victories. If we can stand on our own two feet, why give thanks to the beans and the corn? Yet the notion that we can be completely independent or self-made denies the reality of our reliance on other people and on our natural world.

The Haudenosaunee see humans as interconnected parts of a larger web of life, where each being is uniquely valuable. Crops, trees, rivers, and the sun are respected and thanked as fellow beings in a larger community of mutual aid. If you have this view of life, you don't tear down the forests or pollute the rivers. Instead, as their "Basic Call to Consciousness" describes, you accept other life-forms as part of your extended family. "We are shown that our life exists with the tree life, that our well-being depends on the well-being of the Vegetable Life, that we are close relatives of the four-legged beings."[17]

The Haudenosaunee's expressions of thanksgiving are "the words that come before all else" and precede every council meeting. Instead of being reserved for a special day each year, thanksgiving becomes a way of life.

GRATITUDE MOTIVATES US TO ACT FOR OUR WORLD

What is striking about their thanksgiving prayers is that the Haudenosaunee don't focus on possessions or personal good fortune. Rather, the emphasis is on the blessings we all receive because they are part of our natural world. While the expressions of gratitude are delivered spontaneously in people's own words, the order and format follow a traditional structure. A version of the thanksgiving address has been published by the Mohawks, one of the six nations of the Haudenosaunee, and begins like this:

The People

Today we have gathered and we see that the cycles of life continue. We have been given the duty to live in balance and harmony with each other and all living things. So now, we bring our minds together as one as we give greetings and thanks to each other as People.

Now our minds are one.

The Earth Mother

We are all thankful to our Mother, the Earth, for she gives us all that we need for life. She supports our feet as we walk about upon her. It gives us joy that she continues to care for us as she has from the beginning of time.

To our Mother, we send greetings and thanks.

Now our minds are one.[18]

The other verses in turn give thanks to the waters of the world; the fish life in the water; the varied vastness of plant life; the food plants from the garden; the medicine herbs of the world; the animal life; the trees; the birds, "who each day remind us to enjoy and appreciate life"; the four winds; the thunder beings of thunder and lightning, "who bring with them the water that renews life"; our eldest brother, the Sun; our oldest Grandmother, the moon, "who governs the movement of the ocean tides"; the stars "spread across the sky like jewelry"; Enlightened Teachers; the Creator or Great Spirit; and finally to anything forgotten or not yet named. Thanksgivings like this deepen our instinctual knowledge that we belong to a larger web and have an essential role to play in its well-being. As Haudenosaunee Chief Leon Shenandoah said in his address to the General Assembly of the United Nations in 1985, "Every human being has a sacred duty to protect the welfare of our mother earth from whom all life comes."[19]

Different stories give us different purposes. In the Business as Usual model, nearly everything is privatized. The parts of our world remaining outside individual or corporate ownership, such as the air or the oceans, are not seen as our responsibility. Gratitude is viewed as politeness, not necessity. In their "Basic Call to Consciousness," the Haudenosaunee tell a very different story, one in which our well-being depends on our natural world and gratitude keeps us to our purpose of taking care of life. When we forget this, the larger ecology we depend on gets lost from our sight — and the world unravels.

THE MODERN SCIENCE OF GAIA THEORY

The skill side of gratitude involves recognizing and valuing benefits we might have previously ignored. New information makes a difference; our gratitude to others, and our enthusiasm to help them, can suddenly grow if we discover they have done us a great favor. You might think of examples of this from your own life, perhaps times you've felt warmer toward someone after hearing of support provided to you. This same principle holds true in our relationship with our world.

Just as we depend on plants for food, we also rely on them to make air breathable. Our two neighboring planets, Mars and Venus, have atmospheres that would kill us in a few minutes, and we've only recently discovered that Earth's atmosphere used to be similar. Three billion years ago, our planet's air, like that of Mars and Venus, had much more carbon dioxide and hardly any oxygen.[20] Over the next 2 billion years or so, early plant life did us the remarkable service of making our atmosphere breathable by adding an abundance of oxygen and removing much of the carbon dioxide.

Oxygen is a highly reactive gas, which wouldn't normally be expected to exist at levels as high as the 20 percent we have now. It was the chemically unlikely fact that oxygen has remained at this level for hundreds of millions of years that led British scientist James Lovelock to develop the early ideas of Gaia theory. Here is how he described his moment of insight:

An awesome thought came to me. The Earth's atmosphere was an extraordinary and unstable mixture of gases, yet I knew that it was constant in composition over quite long periods of time. Could it be that life on Earth not only made the atmosphere, but also regulated it — keeping it at a constant composition, and at a level favourable for organisms?[21]

The core tenet of Gaia theory is that our planet is a self-regulating system. There's a parallel here to the way our bodies keep arterial oxygen and temperature levels stable or the way termite colonies maintain their internal temperature and humidity. Living systems have the capacity to keep themselves in balance. Gaia theory shows how life looks after itself, different species acting together to maintain the balance of nature. In addition to maintaining oxygen levels, life plays a role in regulating the salinity of the sea and the dynamics of our climate.

As stars grow older, they tend to burn brighter. Because of this, it is estimated that our sun now puts out at least 25 percent more heat than it did when life began on Earth three and a half billion years ago.[22] Yet has our planet also gotten 25 percent hotter? Human life wouldn't exist if it had. And we have plant life to thank for this. By absorbing carbon dioxide, plants reduce the greenhouse effect of this gas, keeping the planetary temperature within a range suitable for complex life such as ours.

GIVING BACK AND GIVING FORWARD

A timber executive once remarked that when he looked at a tree, all he saw was a pile of money on a stump. Compare this with the Haudenosaunee view that trees should be treated with gratitude and respect. If we saw trees as allies that helped us, we would want to become allies to them. This dynamic pulls us into a cycle of regeneration, in which we take what we need to live and also give back.

Because our modern industrialized culture has forgotten this principle of reciprocity, forests continue to shrink and deserts to grow. To counter this unraveling, let's develop an ecological intelligence that recognizes how our personal well-being depends on the well-being of the natural world. Gratitude plays an important role in this.

TRY THIS:
THANKING WHAT SUPPORTS YOU TO LIVE

Next time you see a tree or plant, take a moment to express thanks. With each breath you take in, experience gratitude for the oxygen that would simply not be there save for the magnificent work plants have done in transforming our atmosphere and making it breathable. As you look at all the greenery, bear in mind also that plants, by absorbing carbon dioxide and reducing the greenhouse effect, have saved our world from becoming dangerously overheated. Without plants and all they do for us, we would not be alive today. Consider how you would like to express your thanks.

The carbon dioxide released when we burn fossil fuels puts back into the atmosphere the gas that ancient plants removed hundreds of millions of years ago. By burning fossil fuels we are reversing one of the planet's cooling mechanisms, and temperatures are rising. Present-day forests make their contribution to planetary cooling not just through absorbing carbon dioxide but also through helping clouds to form. When tropical forests are chopped down, the local climate becomes hotter and drier, making it more difficult for trees to grow again. Tropical forests like the Amazon are under threat not only from deforestation but also from drought related to climate change. They need our help, just as we need theirs.

Much of the oxygen we breathe comes from plants that died long ago. We can give thanks to these ancestors of our present-day foliage, but we can't give back to them. We can, however, give forward. When we are unable to return a favor, we can pay it forward to someone or something else.[23] Using this approach, we can see ourselves as part of a larger flow of giving and receiving throughout time. Receiving from the past, we can give to the future. When tackling issues such as climate change, the stance of gratitude is a refreshing alternative to guilt or fear as a source of motivation.

CHAPTER FOUR

Honoring Our Pain for the World

*P*arsifal, a popular knight in the court of King Arthur, was out on a quest and found himself riding for days through a strange, devastated region, a wasteland where nothing grew. Searching for food and shelter, he came to a lake, where he saw two figures fishing from a boat, one of them dressed in royal garments.

"Where can I find lodging?" Parsifal called out.

The regally dressed fellow, who was the Fisher King, invited him to stay at his castle nearby and gave directions. Before long, Parsifal found himself at the great castle of the Fisher King. Welcomed by courtiers, Parsifal was escorted to a hall where a ceremonial banquet was under way. There, on a kind of hammock bed, lay the king, who appeared to be in great pain from a wound in his groin.

The king was victim of a spell that had stopped his wound from healing. This spell had taken from the ruler and his lands the powers of regeneration. Yet as the evening wore on, no one in the court made mention of the horror they faced.

It was known to them, however, that the spell might be broken if and when a knight appeared and asked the king a compassionate question. But Parsifal had been brought up to believe that it was rude, even out of order, to ask questions of people in authority. So even though he approached the king to greet him, and could smell the foul stench of his wound, he acted as if nothing was wrong.

The next morning, Parsifal woke up to find that the king, his courtiers, and the entire castle had disappeared. Setting off, he eventually found his way out of the wasteland and made it back to King Arthur's court. A feast was held to mark the return of this much-admired knight. The celebration was interrupted by the dramatic entrance of a hideous but wise witch called Cundrie. She publicly scolded Parsifal for lacking the compassion to ask about the suffering of the Fisher King and his people.

"You call yourself a knight," Cundrie cried out. "Look at you! You didn't even have the guts to ask what was going on."

Haunted by Cundrie's accusations and his own feelings of failure, Parsifal fell into a depression. He finally realized he had to return to the court of the Fisher King. It took many years, and many adventures, to find the mysterious castle again. When he did, he found the king in a state of even greater suffering.

This time Parsifal strode right up to the king and knelt before him. "My lord, what aileth thee?" he asked. That Parsifal cared enough to ask this question had an immediate and powerful effect. Color returned to the cheeks of the king, who rose from his couch, his health regained. In the same moment, the wasteland began once again to bloom. The spell was broken.

Parsifal's story, which is part of the legend of the Holy Grail, was put into writing more than eight hundred years ago.[1] Yet the situation it describes, one of great suffering not being acknowledged and of people carrying on as if nothing were wrong, is easily recognizable today. The question "What aileth thee?" or its modern equivalent, "What troubles you?" invites people to express their concern and anguish. There are all kinds of reasons why this question doesn't get asked, and why, like Parsifal, we sometimes find ourselves caught up in the pretense that all is well, even when we know it isn't. When this happens in relation to the state of our world, as it so often does, our survival response becomes blocked. This chapter explores what gets in the way of acknowledging disturbing realities and looks at how honoring our pain for the world can break the spell that maintains Business as Usual.

UNDERSTANDING THE BLOCKED RESPONSE

A key survival mechanism in our response to danger is the activation of alarm. A fire chief once remarked that when a building burns, the people most at risk are not those who panic, who tend to get out quickly, but those who, not having grasped the emergency, sort through their possessions deciding which to save. With this in mind, psychologists Bibb Latané and John Darley carried out a study examining factors that influence our response to potential danger.[2]

In the study volunteer subjects were asked to wait in a room and fill out a questionnaire. While they were at work, a steady stream of smokelike vapor started pouring in through a vent in the wall and filling the room. If individuals were in the room alone, they responded quickly, leaving the room and looking for help. But when several people sat in the room together, they looked to see how others responded. If they saw others remaining calm and continuing to fill in their questionnaires, they were more likely to do so too. Even when the room became so smoky that it was difficult to see, and some subjects were coughing or rubbing their eyes, most persisted with their questionnaires. More than two-thirds continued for a full six minutes before they were "rescued" by one of the researchers.

This experiment serves as a metaphor for our responses to planetary emergency. If the smoke represents disturbing information, filling out the questionnaire is like continuing with Business as

Usual. If we are to survive as a species, we need to understand how our active responses to danger get blocked and also how we can prevent this from happening. What gets in our way of noticing the smoke? Often we experience an inner tension between the impulse to do something and the resistance to it. There are many varieties of resistance. Here are seven common ones:

1. I don't believe it's that dangerous.

When the researchers interviewed the people who had not responded to the smoke, a common reason given by the subjects was that they didn't believe there was a fire. They had developed another explanation for the smoke that led them to discount it as a cause of alarm. That this happened so much more when the subjects saw others ignoring the smoke demonstrates how powerfully influenced we are by what we see others doing. We see this same dynamic at play with global events as well: if we learn some disturbing information about an issue but see most people acting as if it is no big deal, then it is easier to believe the problem can't be that serious.

Corporate-controlled media amplifies this effect. How often, for example, have you seen characters in TV soaps, sitcoms, or dramas express concern about the condition of our world? Most major television stations and newspapers are owned by a tiny number of corporations, and their main source of revenue is advertising. Their commercial goal is to present audiences to advertisers. People are allowed to be disturbed by world events just enough to keep them interested but not so much as to put them off from buying things. As a result, crucial information about the unraveling of our world is omitted or downplayed in news reports. When, for example, the World Meteorological Organization announced in December 2009 that the decade 2000–2009 was on track to be the warmest on record, the managing editor of Fox News sent the following email directive to news teams and producers:

We should refrain from asserting that the planet has warmed (or cooled) in any given period without IMMEDIATELY pointing out that such theories are based upon data that critics have called into question. It is not our place as journalists to assert such notions as facts.[3]

2. It isn't my role to sort this out.

The individualism of Business as Usual creates a sharp dividing line between our problems and those of other people and an even sharper line between the concerns of humans and those of other species. "What happens to polar bears is really not my responsibility," said Martin, a neighbor, when discussing climate change. This fragmentation of responsibility, with its diminishing care for our world, is the dominant mode in industrialized societies. In this view, the world is divided into separate pieces, and we're only responsible for the pieces we own, control, or inhabit. We may take great care of our backyards but view anything beyond the end of the street as someone else's problem.

3. I don't want to stand out from the crowd.

When Joanna first heard the shocking news that President Kennedy had been assassinated, she was standing in the checkout line at a supermarket. Although the radio announcement had been clearly audible, people carried on shopping as if nothing had happened. Joanna, like everyone else, remained passively in line without speaking. Despite her inner response of shock and horror, she kept quiet because she didn't want to stand out from the crowd.

If we're alarmed by something but no one else seems to be, then we risk drawing attention to ourselves if we express our concern. Keeping quiet protects us from the discomfort of standing out. This invisible pressure to conform is both subtle and powerful. It can even lead us to doubt our perceptions, for if no one else is acknowledging a problem, perhaps we've got it wrong.

By naming an issue, we bring it into the open. By doing so we disturb the status quo, since it is more difficult to ignore a problem once it has been acknowledged. Whistle-blowers are often blamed for the inconvenience of being forced to address previously ignored problems. When speaking out is risky, a climate of fear can lead to a culture of collusion. Tony, a participant in one of our courses, described his experience of working in a large corporation: "In my work, it is common practice to leave your conscience at the door. Questioning company policy is viewed as disloyalty; it could threaten your career." Especially at a time of job insecurity, the fear of being labeled a troublemaker discourages the expression of alarm and disturbing information.

4. This information threatens my commercial or political interests.

Throughout the 1990s Thailand's chief meteorologist, Mr. Smith Thammasaroj, gave repeated warnings about the risk of a tsunami to the country's southwest coast.[4] For decades he had studied the relationship between underwater earthquakes and these giant tidal waves; he was so concerned that he recommended beachside hotels in the coastal provinces of Phuket, Phang Nga, and Krabi be fitted with tsunami alarms. His cautions were seen as harmful to the tourist trade, he was sidelined from his job, and his recommendations were ignored. On December 26, 2004, an underwater earthquake off Sumatra led to a massive tsunami striking the very regions he had warned about. In one of the worst disasters in recorded history, more than 5,000 died in Thailand and more than 225,000 in thirteen other countries.

Before the tsunami struck, Mr Thammasaroj, accused of scaremongering, was even banned from some of the provinces he had been trying to protect. One way we resist information we don't want to hear is to attack its source. The tobacco industry did this for decades, with well-funded campaigns to discredit both the science and the scientists proving that smoking killed people. Even though internal memos show the industry knew the science was correct, they still sought to invalidate research findings that clashed with their commercial interests.[5] Public-relations companies were paid millions to cast doubt on the link between tobacco and health problems. The same thing is happening today with the science of climate change; oil and gas companies spent an astonishing $169 million in 2009 on lobbying in the United States.[6]

5. It is so upsetting that I prefer not to think about it.

While human history has seen its share of disasters, what's different these days is our trajectory. As our world continues to heat up, it is horrifying to consider where this is leading. So why is the dominant response to continue with Business as Usual? One reason is that our planetary emergency can feel too painful even to look at. Here are some of the comments made by people we interviewed. From Isabelle, mother of two young children: "I used to be politically active, but these days I can't bear to listen to the news because I find it so depressing." And from John, grandparent: "I know the world's a mess, but I don't want to be constantly reminded of it. I prefer not to think about it."

6. I feel paralyzed. I'm aware of the danger, but I don't know what to do.

How can we begin to tackle our problems if we find them too painful even to think about? Yet being aware of the problems and not knowing how to respond can be even more agonizing. Here is how Jennifer, who'd been an activist for many years, described her experience:

In the 1990s, I'd felt optimistic; I sensed people were waking up, that there was a growing determination to do something. But it didn't come to much, and the problems we face just seem to get worse. I feel I must do something; I can't just watch this. Yet there is so much that needs doing, I don't know where to start. It is overwhelming, and I feel paralyzed.

7. There's no point doing anything, since it won't make any difference.

What if we're too late? What if we've already done so much damage that our world is dying and our industrialized society, like the *Titanic*, is sinking? This perspective makes it hard to find authentic meaning and purpose in life. On the one hand, we recognize the Business as Usual mode as living a lie, yet on the other, attempts to bring positive change are viewed with cynicism and seen as peddling false optimism. What remains is a story of decline, of going through the motions of living, making the best of what we have before the final collapse.

Though this outlook seems bleak, a recent study by the Mental Health Foundation suggests that such feelings are widespread. In a survey of more than two thousand people, one in four said they were less inclined to plan for the future, and one in seven said they were reluctant to have children because of world conditions.[7] More than half described feeling powerless to change things, and 30 percent said that nothing helped relieve their worries about the future.

WORKING WITH OUR DESPAIR FOR THE WORLD

We live in extraordinary times, and we can be caught between contrasting versions of reality. The first four resistances grow out of the Business as Usual story that doesn't recognize the crisis; the last three are linked to the ghastly realization that things are so much worse than we'd thought.

We can exist in both these realities at the same time — going about our normal lives in the mode of Business as Usual while also remaining painfully aware of the multifaceted crisis unfolding around us. Living in this double reality creates a split in our mind. It is as though one part of our brain operates on the default assumption that things are fine, while another part knows full well they are not. One way of dealing with the confusion and agony of this splitting is to push the crisis out of view. This is like carrying on with the questionnaire and trying not to think about the smoke. But this way of living is difficult to sustain, particularly as the condition of our world continues to worsen.

It is difficult even to talk about this. There are taboos in normal conversation that block the discussion of anything considered too depressing. When we feel dread about what may lie ahead, outrage at what is happening to our planet, or sadness about what has already been lost, it is likely that we have nowhere to take these feelings. As a result, we tend to keep them to ourselves and suffer in isolation. If people see us keeping quiet, not mentioning the crisis, then just like in the smoke-filled room, they'll be more likely to keep their mouths shut as well. Yet if we reveal our distress, and name the horrors we see, we're likely to be called overly negative or too emotional.

We can be caught between two fears — the fear of what will happen if we, as a society, continue the way we're going and the fear of acknowledging how bad things are because of the despair that doing so brings up. If we listen to the first fear, it can provoke responses that aid our survival; but to benefit from this wake-up call, we need to free ourselves from the stifling effect of the second fear. There are ways to do this.

More than thirty years ago, an approach was developed that

helps people respond creatively to world crises rather than feeling overwhelmed or paralyzed by distress. As with grief work, facing our distress doesn't make it disappear. Instead, when we do face it, we are able to place our distress within a larger landscape that gives it a different meaning. Rather than feeling afraid of our pain for the world, we learn to feel strengthened by it.

When first developed by Joanna in the late 1970s, this approach, which largely involves working with groups in a structured workshop format, was known as "despair and empowerment work." Because it deepens our relationship with the web of life, the term "deep ecology workshops" has also been used. Since the late 1990s, this approach has been known as the Work That Reconnects. The principles and practices can be applied not just to workshops but also to education, psychotherapy, community organizing, and spiritual practice. At the heart of this approach lies a different way of thinking about our pain for the world.

PAIN FOR THE WORLD IS NORMAL, HEALTHY, AND WIDESPREAD

Many years ago, a therapist told Joanna that her concerns about bulldozers flattening the forests stemmed from her fear of her libido. This tendency to reduce our distress about planetary conditions to some kind of psychological problem or neurosis is common. Our anguish and alarm about what we're doing to our world are viewed as symptoms to be treated or as markers of an underlying personal issue. Self-help groups have not been immune to this approach: a recovering alcoholic, mentioning his fears for our world in his support group, found himself challenged with the question, "What are you running away from in your own life that you bring up such concerns?"

Drawing on her doctoral studies exploring convergences between Buddhist philosophy and systems theory, Joanna saw that the meaning we give to our emotional responses is of central importance. The perception of radical interconnectedness found in both Buddhism and systems thinking supports a reframing of our distress about world conditions. It helps us recognize how healthy a reaction this distress is and how necessary it is for our survival. A central principle of the Work That Reconnects is that *pain for the world*, a phrase that covers a range of feelings, including outrage, alarm, grief, guilt, dread, and despair, is a normal, healthy response to a world in trauma.

In Buddhism, as in other major world religions, open alertness that allows our heart to be stirred by the suffering of others is appreciated as a strength. Indeed, in every spiritual tradition, compassion, which literally means "to suffer with," is prized as an essential and noble capacity. This ability is evidence of our interconnectedness with all life.

The concept of "negative feedback loops" from systems theory helps us recognize how this ability to suffer with our world is essential for our survival. We navigate through life by paying attention to information, or feedback, that tells us when we are off course and by responding with a course correction. This dynamic process loops continually: stray off course, notice this, make a response that brings us back on course, stray off course again, notice this, come back on course (see Fig. 4). Since this process functions to diminish the degree to which one is off course, it is called a negative feedback loop.

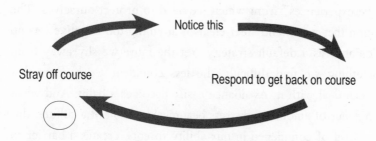

Figure 4. A negative feedback loop:
Each response reduces deviation from chosen course.

It is through loops like this that living systems keep themselves in balance. For example, if we feel too cold, we might respond by putting on a jacket. If after a while we feel too hot, we take the jacket off. If a roomful of people start to feel too hot, someone might open a window. In this case, the system of the group acts through its members to keep the room temperature comfortable.

How would we notice if we were straying off course as a society? We would start to feel uncomfortable. If we were heading in a dangerous direction, we might feel alarmed; if something unacceptable was taking place, we might feel outrage. If parts of our world that we loved were dying, we would expect to grieve. These feelings are normal, healthy responses. They help us notice what's going on; they are also what rouses our response.

UNBLOCKING FEEDBACK RELEASES ENERGY

In our workshops we see people sharing their anguish and despair for our world situation and then emerging energized and nourished by the experience. That facing painful feelings can enliven people like this flies in the face of common assumptions about how best to deal with distress.

There's a strong current in mainstream culture that views depressing news, gloomy thoughts, and feelings of distress as "negative experiences" from which we need to protect ourselves. The notion that we should steer clear of anything too negative sets up avoidance as a default strategy. Yet the more we shy away from something we find difficult, the less confident we become that we can deal with it. Avoidance easily becomes a habit. And when avoidance of emotional distress becomes the habit of a culture, this low level of confidence in our ability to cope creates a barrier to publicly acknowledging upsetting information. This in turn leads to a selective screening out of aspects of reality that seem too painful to bear, too distressing to contemplate.

The disturbing realities of early twenty-first-century Earth, along with what we are likely to face over the coming decades, far exceed any previous experience of disaster in our history. It is not surprising that the feelings provoked by this reality are difficult to bear. "If I open the door to those feelings," said a friend in recent conversation, "I'll be plunged to a place so low I don't think I'll ever get back." What makes many of us nervous about looking at our grief or despair is the fear that we will become stuck in those emotions. A key issue here is our capacity to deal with distress.

Emotional distress can be motivating, but if it goes beyond what we imagine we can cope with, we may just shut down. While on the outside we may appear to be holding it together, when we close off emotionally we feel less alive, our energy sagging and our sensitivity dulled. We may feel we're just going through the motions. Alcohol, drugs, shopping, and antidepressants are among the devices we use to keep distress under wraps. In the short term, these salves can seem effective. But as we become dependent on them, our society continues to stray off course and our world becomes a wasteland.

The Work That Reconnects offers a different way forward. In its workshop form, it offers a safe, supportive forum where distress can be voiced, heard, and valued, thus unblocking the feedback loop. As one participant said:

> *I want to face the truth of what's happening in our world. If that truth is painful, then I need to face the pain.*

It is our consistent experience that as people open to the flow of their emotional experience, including despair, sadness, guilt, fury, or fear, they feel a weight being lifted from them. In the journey into the pain, something foundational shifts; a turning occurs.

When we touch into our depths, we find that the pit is not bottomless. When people are able to tell the truth about what they know, see, and feel is happening to their world, a transformation occurs. There is an increased determination to act and a renewed appetite for life.[8]

A range of factors acts together to bring about this shift. First, as noted, repressing emotions and information dampens our energy. It is enlivening to go with, rather than against, the flow of our deep-felt responses to the world. Second, we feel tremendous relief on realizing our solidarity with others. Two other factors play a crucial role. One concerns the process by which we integrate painful information, and the other relates to what pain for the world reveals about the nature of the self.

INFORMATION IS NOT ENOUGH

Environmental and social change organizations often fall into the trap of assuming that if only people knew how bad things were, they would become active in tackling the issues. So the emphasis falls on presenting information and arguments, backing these up with shocking facts, graphs, and images. This raising of awareness is important and necessary — but what happens when people are already feeling so overwhelmed they don't feel they can cope with any more distress? Or if they believe they need to protect themselves from negative thinking? In these cases, presenting more shocking facts can just increase the resistance.

Elisabeth Kübler-Ross, a doctor known for her work with people suffering from life-threatening conditions, described a process of coming to terms with bad news that involves a number of stages.[9] In the beginning, the loss doesn't feel real. Someone may acknowledge that something has happened but act as if this hasn't yet been accepted. The information may be taken in on a superficial level but not yet digested.

In his classic text on grief counseling, psychology professor J. William Worden identifies the initial tasks of grieving as first accepting the loss and second feeling the pain of grief.[10] When we feel this emotion, we know not only that the loss is real but also that it matters to us. That's the digestion phase — where the awareness sinks to a deeper place within us so that we take in what it means. Only then can we find a way forward that is based on an accurate perception of reality.

There is a journey to really getting it that our planet faces a life-threatening condition. If we haven't fully taken in and digested the bad news of our planetary predicament, then we might see little reason to step outside the story of Business as Usual. But if the disturbing diagnosis of unraveling has really landed inside us, then we know we can't go back to pretending that all is well.

Each day we lose valuable parts of our biosphere as species become extinct and ecosystems destroyed — yet where is their funeral service? If our world is dying piece by piece without our publicly and collectively expressing our grief, we might easily assume that these losses aren't important. Honoring our pain for the world is a way of valuing our awareness, first, that we have noticed, and second, that we care. Intellectual awareness by itself is not enough. We need to digest the bad news. That is what rouses us to respond.

So what helps us digest the information we're already aware of? A starting point is just to hear ourselves speak what we already know. By giving voice to our concerns, we bring them into the open. Within the workshops, a paired listening exercise called "open sentences" is often used to facilitate this.

TRY THIS: OPEN SENTENCES ON CONCERN

Sit in pairs, with one partner acting as listener and the other as speaker. The role of the listener is to listen attentively without saying anything. The speaker talks for two minutes or so for each of the following open sentences, saying the first part of the sentence and continuing to say whatever seems to naturally follow. If not sure what to say, the person talking can come back to the beginning of the sentence and start again, seeing what naturally follows each time. Swap roles after each sentence or all four so that both partners hear each other.

1. When I think about the condition of our world, I would say things are getting...
2. Some concerns I have include...
3. Some feelings that come up when I think about these are...
4. What I do with these feelings is...

Some unspoken rules govern the content and emotional bandwidth of normal conversations. If we stray too far outside agreeable territory, for example, by raising an issue seen as too disturbing or by expressing a feeling with too much intensity, we are likely to be met by responses that close down our expression. We might find ourselves caught up in an argument or see the issue ignored as conversation is steered back to more comfortable topics. To address the challenges we face, we need to develop ways of talking about them that don't become battles about who is to blame or an avoidance mechanism that filters out the true depths of our concern. By giving each speaker space to talk without interruption, the open sentences process makes room for a different kind of conversation to take place.

This simple exercise often brings up strong feelings. Yet the process is not about *making* people feel something; rather, it is about uncovering what is already there. It is making space to hear one another, to explore our own responses, to allow what's under the surface to be expressed. When we allow feelings to move through us, we are less likely to get stuck in them.

When we experience pain for the world, the world is feeling through us. This is a central insight of the work: if feelings flow into us from the world, they can also flow back out again — they don't have to get stuck in us. A process called Breathing Through, adapted from an ancient Buddhist meditation for developing compassion, reinforces this understanding.

TRY THIS: BREATHING THROUGH

Closing your eyes, focus on your breathing. Don't try to breathe in any special way, slow or long. Just watch the breathing as it happens, in and out.

Note the accompanying sensations at the nostrils or in the chest or abdomen. Stay passive and alert, like a cat by a mouse hole. . . .

As you watch the breathing, note that it happens by itself, without your will, without your deciding each time to inhale or exhale. It's as though you're being breathed — being breathed by life. Just as everyone in this room, in this city, on this planet now, is being breathed by life, sustained in a vast living breathing web. . . .

Now visualize your breath as a stream or ribbon of air. See it flow up through your nose, down through your windpipe, and into your lungs. Now take it through the heart. Picture it flowing through your heart and out through an opening there to reconnect with the larger web of life. Let the breath-stream, as it passes through you and through your heart, appear as one loop within that vast web, connecting you with it....

Now open your awareness to the suffering in the world. For now drop all defenses and open to your knowledge of that suffering. Let it come as concretely as you can...images of your fellow beings in pain and need, in fear and isolation, in prisons, hospitals, tenements, refugee camps... no need to strain for these images; they are present to you by virtue of our interexistence. Relax and just let them surface...the countless hardships of our fellow human beings, and of our animal brothers and sisters as well, as they swim the seas and fly the air of this planet...Now breathe in the pain like granules of sand on the stream of air, up through your nose, down through your trachea, lungs and heart, and out again into the world...You are asked to do nothing for now, but let it pass through your heart...Be sure that stream flows through and out again, don't hang on to that pain...Surrender it for now to the healing resources of life's vast web.

"Let all sorrows ripen in me," said Shantideva, the Buddhist saint. We help them ripen by passing them through our hearts...making good, rich compost out of all that grief...so we can learn from it, enhancing our larger, collective knowing...

If no images or feelings arise and there is only blankness, gray and numb, breathe that through. The numbness itself is a very real part of our world.

And if what surfaces for you is not pain for other beings

so much as losses and hurts in your own life, breathe those through too. Your own difficulties are an integral part of the grief of our world, and arise with it....

Should you fear that with this pain your heart might break, remember that the heart that breaks open can hold the whole universe. Your heart is that large. Trust it. Keep breathing.

A DIFFERENT VIEW OF SELF

The Vietnamese Zen master Thich Nhat Hanh was once asked what we need to do to save our world. "What we most need to do," he replied, "is to hear within us the sounds of the Earth crying."[11] The idea of the Earth crying within us, or through us, doesn't make sense if we view ourselves only as separate individuals. Yet if we think of ourselves as deeply embedded in a larger web of life, as Gaia theory, Buddhism, and many other, especially indigenous, spiritual traditions suggest, then the idea of the world feeling through us seems entirely natural.

This view of the self is very different from that found in the Business as Usual model. Its extreme individualism takes each of us as a separate bundle of self-interest, with motivations and emotions that only make sense within the confines of our own stories. Pain for the world tells a different story, one about our interconnectedness. We feel distress when other beings suffer because, at a deep level, we are not separate from them. The isolation that splits us from the living body of our world is an illusion; the pain breaks through it to tell us who we really are.

What we see happening in these workshops is more than just people learning not to fear their pain for the world, more than just the building of community and the unblocking of feedback. We witness a profound shift in people's relationships with the world, bringing a deep and nourishing sense of connection.

Daniel, a physician, said, "I never felt I belonged anywhere before. Now I know I belong to this world, and in my bones I feel I am part of it." Annie, a schoolteacher, added, "After the workshop, I remember feeling an uncommon and wonderful sense that I do have a place in the world."

Our pain for the world arises out of our interexistence with all life. When we hear the sounds of the Earth crying within us, we're unblocking not just feedback but also the channels of felt connectedness that join us with our world. These channels act like a root system, opening us to a source of strength and resilience as old and enduring as life itself.

In the process, the view that we are separate from our world falls away. The term *deep ecology*, coined by Norwegian ecophilosopher Arne Naess, captures the essence of this shift.[12] When we perceive our deeper identity as an ecological self that includes not just us but also all life on Earth, then acting for the sake of our world doesn't seem like a sacrifice. It seems a natural thing to do.

PERSONAL PRACTICES TO HONOR
OUR PAIN FOR THE WORLD

Open Sentences and the Parsifal Question

A starting point for exploring your emotional reactions to world conditions is simply to ask yourself how you feel. The Parsifal question, adapted for this context, involves asking yourself, "What troubles me about what's happening in our world?" then making room to listen to your response. You can draw out your responses more by writing them down. Whenever you're not sure what to say or write, you can use the open sentences technique to give you a starting point, and then continue the sentence with whatever naturally flows. The open sentences on page 72 offer a useful launching point for reflection or personal journaling. Some other open sentences we often use in workshops are:

- When I imagine the world we will leave our children, it looks like...
- One of my worst fears about the future is...
- The feelings about this that I carry around with me are...
- Ways I avoid these feelings include...
- Some ways I can use these feelings are...

Each is a springboard into territory usually excluded from conversation. When we bring our fears into the open, they lose their power to haunt us. Jade, a young woman attending one of our workshops, described the impact this had on her:

Previously I'd been terrified of the prospect of global and ecological collapse. It was so horrifying a thought that I couldn't face it. It was too much to look at world problems, so I tried to shut them out.

At that workshop, things changed. I faced my horrors and remember thinking "this is my terror and it is really bad." Previously I'd been really afraid, but afterward my nightmares stopped. I felt more accepting, putting things in perspective better, thinking that we just do our best, so I got on with it.

After the workshop, Jade left her job and started working for an environmental organization. Facing the awfulness had strengthened her resolve to find and play her part in addressing her concerns about the world.

Breathing Through

The Breathing Through meditation described on pages 73–75 helps bring feelings to the surface; it can also become a trusted ally if you fear becoming overwhelmed. Bringing your attention back to your breath has a stabilizing effect, as does remembering the image of feelings coming in, passing through your heart, and then being released into the healing resources of the web of life.

Creative Expression of Our Pain for the World

If we are not used to articulating our emotions, it can sometimes be difficult to know what we feel. A way of drawing out feelings so that they become easier to recognize is to give them a form, such as a shape or color on paper, a sound with your voice, or a texture with clay. Moving beyond words, or diving beneath them, takes us to that subliminal level where we sense threats so that we can touch into and release our deeper responses to the condition of our world.

TRY THIS: DRAWING OUT YOUR CONCERNS

Take a blank piece of paper and some colored pens. Scribble, doodle, or draw any images to represent concerns you have and the feelings that accompany them.

When images surface, they allow us to step into the realm of our intuitive responses to our planet-time. We may be surprised by what our hands portray, images of concern revealed on paper that we may not have spoken or even been aware of. Images, once birthed, have a reality of their own that we don't need to explain or defend or apologize for. They just are as they are, showing what they show and bringing into view more than words alone might do.

Using Ceremony

Most cultures honor significant emotions, such as grief following the death of a loved one or gratitude at times of thanksgiving, by marking them with ceremonies or forms of symbolic representation. We can honor our feelings of pain for the world by developing our own ceremonies to mark them.

TRY THIS: A PERSONAL CAIRN OF MOURNING

What is being lost in our world that you mourn for? While holding this question in your mind and heart, go for a walk and look for an object that represents something precious our world is losing. Find a special place to lay this object to rest as a way of acknowledging the loss and the grief you feel. You can return to this special place to mark other losses, over time building a small pile, or cairn, of objects symbolizing what is being lost.

This cairn of mourning is a marker affirming that you've noticed and that you care.

If we felt the pain of loss each time an ecosystem was destroyed, a species wiped out, or a child killed by war or starvation, we wouldn't be able to continue living the way we do. It would tear us apart inside. The losses continue because they aren't registered, they aren't marked, they aren't seen as important. By choosing to honor the pain of loss rather than discounting it, we break the spell that numbs us to the dismantling of our world.

The Power of Conversations

An expression we've often heard is "I didn't realize I felt so strongly until I heard myself say that." By speaking our concerns, and giving voice to our feelings, we make them more visible not just to others but also to ourselves. The more we draw issues into the open, the more inclined we become to tackle them. As best-selling author Margaret Wheatley observes:

> Many large-scale change efforts — some of which have won the Nobel Peace Prize — began with the simple but courageous act of friends talking to one another about their fears and dreams. In reviewing a number of these efforts and how they began, I always found a phrase: "Some friends and I started talking..." [13]

When people reveal to us their anguish about world conditions, our response powerfully influences the way the conversation develops. Recognizing the sharing of pain for the world as a crucial communication, we can honor its expression by giving our full attention. Rather than attempting to fix feelings of distress, we accept their validity and significance. Doing this is in itself an act for the Great Turning.

Seeking Support/Workshops/Practice Groups

A particular kind of magic happens when the Work That Reconnects is applied in a group setting. It is tremendously reassuring to find we are not alone in feeling pain for our world. To name it as normal is itself a healing act. See the resources section in the back of the book to find out about workshops near you.

Another way of treading the journey of the spiral with others is to form a support, practice, or study group based on reading this book together or drawing on the other resources listed on page 255.

Pain for the World as a Call to Adventure

There comes a point in many adventure stories when the main characters have seen the true nature of the crisis they face and it is far worse that they'd previously imagined. It is not just their own lives that are at stake but also a community they belong to, a value they cherish, a cause larger than themselves. With the limited tools and resources available to them, it might seem that they don't stand much chance. To have any hope at all, they need to step out onto new ground in a quest to find the allies, understandings, and tools that will help.

We will have moments when the penny really drops that our world is in grave danger. When facing a challenge far beyond what we might normally think ourselves capable of dealing with, we need to move beyond the familiar and learn the art of seeing with new eyes. The next section of this book introduces four empowering shifts in perception. We like to think of these as the four discoveries: a wider sense of self, a different kind of power, a richer experience of community, and a larger view of time.

PART TWO

Seeing with New Eyes

CHAPTER FIVE

A Wider Sense of Self

In a fictional future on a faraway world, the indigenous Na'vi have developed such a richly satisfying life of connectedness that they can't be bought off. Preserving the beauty and vitality of their world is more important to them than anything a materialistic society can offer. This story, familiar to anyone who has seen the film *Avatar*, is set on a fertile moon called Pandora. The events the film portrays are recognizable on our planet too. Beautiful forests are being torn down to make way for open-cast mines, while corporate-backed mercenaries crush opposition from the local population.

At the start of an epic adventure, the central characters often appear poorly equipped for the challenge they face. Whether it is David facing Goliath or Frodo bearing the ring, the hero of the story seems hopelessly underpowered for the role he or she steps forward to play. We can feel like that too. "Who am I to take on the problems of the world?" we might ask. Yet our view of what we're capable of is linked to our sense of who and what we are. Discovering hidden depths to our identity opens up a whole new set of possibilities. In *Avatar*, Jake Sully makes this journey, starting out as a loyal servant of the corporation and gradually finding himself a defender of the world he has joined. This chapter explores how we can experience a comparable transformation, in which the emergence of a wider sense of self powerfully enhances our ability to contribute to our world.

TRANSFORMING SELFISHNESS

People often despair about the problem of human selfishness. If, as some believe, we are genetically programmed to put our comfort and convenience before the interests of others or our world, then the outlook is pretty dismal. But what if we could transform the expression of selfishness by widening and deepening the self for whom we act? Arne Naess issued this invitation when he wrote:

> Unhappily, the extensive moralizing within the ecological movement has given the public the false impression that they are being asked to make a sacrifice — to show more responsibility, more concern and a nicer moral standard. But all of that would flow naturally and easily if the self were widened and deepened so that protection of nature was felt and perceived as protection of our very selves.[1]

Many of us may remember special moments when we have felt unusually connected to the world around us. Perhaps we were enthralled by a glimpse of great beauty, or we witnessed an event so remarkable it took our breath away. "I have been a recipient of an unmistakable grace," wrote author Sam Keen, describing the time he spent out in the woods watching two bobcats sitting on a log singing in the night.[2] These cherished moments, which some would describe as spiritual experiences, nourish us. They pull us out of preoccupation with our personal details and into a larger, more mysterious, and magical experience of being alive.

By inviting in these experiences of interconnectedness we can enhance our sense of belonging to our world. This mode of being widens and deepens our sense of who we are.

DIFFERENT VIEWS OF THE SELF

When author and filmmaker Helena Norberg-Hodge first visited the mountainous region of Ladakh in northern India, she was struck by how happy the people were.[3] Even though the physical conditions were challenging, with villages cut off by snow for many months each year, the villagers had a rich and satisfying way of life that met their basic needs well. Though the villages she visited had no electricity, the villagers' highly developed cooperative culture ensured that everyone had enough food, clothes, and shelter. There was hardly any crime, depression was rare, and suicides were virtually unheard of. That was in the mid-1970s.

Since then, the picture has changed. With huge billboard advertisements in the towns glamorizing the path to material prosperity, many of the younger generation have left the villages in search of employment. While some now have motorcycles and television sets, there have also been suicides, even among school-age children. Previously, success and failure had largely been shared experiences, with villagers working together to succeed in tasks like bringing in a harvest. The modern consumer culture, however, has brought in its wake the rat race that divides people into winners and losers, with constant pressure to come out on top.

The extreme individualism of industrialized countries is so well established that some regard it as our natural state. Seeing it emerge as a fairly new phenomenon in Ladakh is a reminder that the desire to put ourselves first isn't a fixed feature of human nature. Rather, it is a product of a particular way of understanding the self that arises out of our cultural context.

There are many different ways of viewing the self. The concept of a separate self, a discrete entity separate from other people and the world, is only one way. This separate individual self, or "ego," as it is sometimes called, has a clear outer boundary. This isn't all of us, though, as Carl Jung once wrote: "It is a remarkable fact that a life lived entirely from the ego is dull not only for the person himself but for all concerned."[4]

The following exercise offers an opportunity to explore who else we are besides just our ego self.

TRY THIS: TELL ME, WHO ARE YOU?

This process can be done alone or with a partner.

By yourself: Imagine encountering a stranger who's keen to get to know you and who asks, "Tell me, who are you?" Write your reply in a notebook. Whenever you finish a response, imagine being asked the same question again. And again. See if you can respond a different way each time, writing down whatever answer feels right, and then repeating the process. Aim for at least ten different responses. If you're feeling curious, see if you can fill a whole page.

With a partner: Take turns, with each of you taking five minutes in each role, one asking, "Tell me, who are you?" and the other replying, repeating this process again and again, allowing whatever words come up. Rest assured that the answers will be different every time.

When doing this process, people are often surprised by how many different ways they see themselves. Even when we describe ourselves us as distinct individuals, our sense of identity also involves a connected self that emerges from our relationships, contexts, and communities. As different aspects of who we are grow more or less pronounced, our sense of self changes over time. Here is how a workshop participant experienced this process.

Throughout his twenties, Tom had seen his main purpose as enjoying life. He wasn't much interested in world issues. He had enough going on in his own life. In his early thirties he got married, and a short while later, his wife became pregnant. The day he saw the ultrasound scan, his whole view of who and what he was changed. There, in front of him, was proof that he had become a father.

For the first time in his life, what happened after he died started to become important to him. He was thinking in a time frame that extended beyond his own life. Tom no longer thought of himself as only a separate individual. He experienced himself to be part of something larger — a family.

Tom has discovered a wider and deeper sense of self. He hasn't stopped being an individual; rather, his personal identity has become rooted in something larger — in this case, the shared identity of his family.

WIDENING CIRCLES OF SELF

When Tom became a parent he grew closer to other members of his and his wife's family, particularly those who helped in the care of their child. In his twenties, he had lost the sense of being part of an extended family. While he had felt independent and free to follow his own desires, he had felt very alone at times and lacking in a meaningful sense of purpose. Reconnecting with his family had restored a sense of belonging. Feeling grateful for the help he was getting, he experienced a sense of kinship that left him wanting to help other family members too.

We don't think of it as altruism when family members help one another, or when parents make sacrifices for the benefit of their children. It is viewed as entirely normal, even taken for granted. In a similar way, when we feel part of a team or a circle of friends, it is natural to give our support without charging by the hour or asking what's in it for us. Arne Naess comments on this cooperative tendency:

Early in life, the social self is sufficiently developed so that we do not prefer to eat a big cake alone. We share the cake with

our family and friends. We identify with these people sufficiently to see our joy in their joy, and to see our disappointment in theirs.[5]

When we identify with something larger than ourselves, whether
that be our family, a circle of friends, a team, or a community, that
becomes part of who we are. There is so much more to us than just a
separate self; our connected self is based on recognizing that we are
part of many larger circles.

In the course of a day, we move between these different expressions of identity. We might inhabit our family self when attending
to relatives, our team self when playing a role at work, our social
self when enjoying a walk home with a friend. If we have a patriotic
moment, that's an expression of our national identity. If we feel a
sense of belonging when viewing a photo of Earth from space, that
reflects the planetary dimension of our connected self. Our sense
of rootedness comes from experiencing these more encompassing
circles of our identity (see Fig. 5).

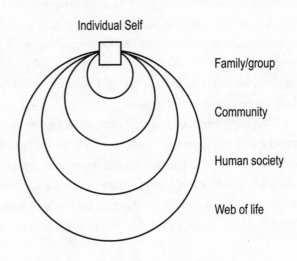

Figure 5. We are part of widening circles.

How we define our self-interest depends on which dimensions of self we are identifying with most strongly in that moment. Psychologist Marilynn Brewer writes, "When the definition of self changes, the meaning of self-interest and self-serving motivations changes accordingly."[6]

The distinction often made between selfishness and altruism is therefore misleading. It is based on a split between self and other, presenting us with a choice between helping ourselves (selfishness) and helping others (altruism). When we consider the connected self, we recognize this choice as nonsense. It is from our connected selves that much of what people most value in life emerges, including love, friendship, loyalty, trust, relationship, belonging, purpose, gratitude, spirituality, mutual aid, and meaning.

The philosopher Immanuel Kant made a distinction between "moral acts" and "beautiful acts."[7] We tend to perform moral acts out of a sense of duty or obligation. In contrast, we perform beautiful acts when we do what is morally right because it is attractive to us, the action motivated more by desire than duty. When our connected sense of self is well developed, we are more often drawn to beautiful acts. When we lose our sense of felt connectedness, we miss out on this sort of beauty, with tragic consequences.

THE PLAGUE OF AFFLUENZA

When people lose their sense of belonging to larger circles, they lose not only the motivation to act for their communities and environment but also valuable sources of support and resilience. Alongside the erosion of extended family and community networks, the rate of depression in industrialized countries has been steadily rising for more than fifty years. It has now reached such epidemic proportions that one in two of us is likely to suffer a significant depressive episode at some point in our lives.

While the hyperindividualism of industrialized countries has deep roots and a long history, it has become more extreme over the past five decades. As discussed, falling trust levels are an indicator of this, with surveys in the United States showing the proportion of people replying yes to the question, "Can most people be trusted?" fell from 56 percent in the mid-1960s to 33 percent in 1995.[8] While recognizing common purposes and shared identities helps build trust, the trend toward increased individualism sets us against each other. Instead of encouraging us to pull together at a time of planetary emergency, the dominant cultural ethic has become one of chasing after personal advantage.

Seeing ourselves as separate entities, rather than as connected parts of a larger whole, reduces the search for purpose to a preoccupation with how well our self is doing compared with others. As a result, the unhealthy obsession with appearance and status known as affluenza, discussed in chapter 3, has become a major contributor to emotional distress. As status has become associated with having more, bigger, and supposedly better things, the desire to keep up appearances propels the consumerism that is wrecking our world.

What we see here is how personal well-being, community well-being, and planetary well-being are linked to the way we view our self. The extreme individualism of our culture is harmful at all three levels. To promote the recovery of our world and the healing of our communities, while also leading lives that are rich and satisfying, we need to embody a larger story of who and what we are.

INTERCONNECTEDNESS IS NOT ABOUT MERGING

Experiencing the wider identity of our connected self does not mean losing our individuality. Quite the opposite: it is through finding and playing our unique role within a community that we feel more strongly part of it. There is an important shift here away from the idea that cohesion and order depend on everyone thinking and acting the same way. That would simply lead to a mob mentality, in which our uniqueness is submerged and our autonomy abandoned.

For a complex system to self-organize and function well, it requires both the integration and the differentiation of its parts. Complex organisms such as our bodies require many different types of cells, and a resilient ecosystem requires high levels of biodiversity. Compare that with monocrop agriculture, in which rows and rows of the same plant growing the same way might look ordered but are dependent on chemical inputs and vulnerable to changing conditions. It is similar with human beings. We don't need to be like the Borg in *Star Trek*, robbed of free will and individuality, to experience ourselves as connected parts of a larger whole. The courage to listen to our conscience and live our own truth is integral to joining, rather than merging, with the larger circles of life we belong to.

When you fall in love, you feel incredibly bonded with your loved one and at the same time more uniquely yourself, different from anyone else in the world. The experience of connectedness with a healthy community has similar qualities; it brings out our latent, distinctive gifts.

RESTORING AND "RESTORYING" CONNECTEDNESS

Rather than viewing our self as a fixed thing with characteristics that can't be changed, we can think of ourselves as a flow of becoming. The static view of self is similar to a picture hanging on a wall, something that is set in a particular way and that resists transformation. Whenever we have thoughts like "I'm not the sort of person who..." we're painting a picture of ourselves like this. An alternative view is to think of each moment as similar to a frame in a movie. If something isn't in the frame right now, that doesn't mean it won't be later. This perspective invites a greater sense of possibility.

We participate in many flows of becoming, from our own life to the lives of our family, community, and world. Each flow can be thought of as a story that moves through the players in it. With our individual self, the plot revolves around our personal adventures, gains, and losses. With our family self, the narrative can be traced back through our ancestors and extends into future generations. If we identify with a particular cultural or religious community, we are part of its story as well.

Arne Naess introduced the term *ecological self* to describe the wider sense of identity that arises when our self-interest includes the natural world.[9] When we include the natural world, we are brought into a much larger story of who and what we are. Recognizing ourselves as part of the living body of Earth opens us to a great source of strength. The expression "act your age" takes on a different meaning when we see ourselves as part of an amazing flow of life that started on this planet more than three and a half billion years ago. We come from an unbroken lineage that has survived through five mass extinctions. Life has a powerful creative energy and manifests a powerful desire to continue. When we align ourselves with the well-being of our world, we allow that desire and creative energy to act through us. When asked how he handles despair, rainforest activist John Seed replied:

> I try to remember that it's not me, John Seed, trying to protect the rainforest. Rather, I am part of the rainforest protecting itself. I am that part of the rainforest recently emerged into human thinking.[10]

The understanding that we are an intrinsic part of the living Earth lies at the heart of indigenous belief systems around the world. Describing the traditional view of the world he grew up with in Malawi, Africa, theologian Harvey Sindima writes, "We live in the web of life in reciprocity with people, other creatures, and the earth, recognizing that they are part of us and we are part of them."[11]

INCREASED CONNECTIVITY IS NO PICNIC

Increasing our felt connectedness with life on Earth will not always bring us ease and harmony. History has shown us many examples of people whose allegiance to wider circles of life impelled them to act in ways that brought discomfort to, and even persecution from, their peers. Gandhi braved the ire of his coreligionists in order to pursue his vision of a united, inclusive India. More recently, Jacque Brever, at the time a single mother in her thirties, fled her home in Boulder, Colorado, and went into hiding after receiving death threats.[12] She had dared to blow the whistle on illegal and highly dangerous practices at the nearby Rocky Flats nuclear facility.

In 1989 the plant's management, Rockwell International, was under investigation, but it seemed impossible to get any insider to talk. Jacque was one of the highly skilled and highly paid "chem ops" workers who operated special incinerators and who, when ordered, conducted secret midnight burnings to get rid of plutonium waste. She decided to speak out. Her testimony to the FBI and the grand jury provided key evidence that helped citizens protect themselves and their homes.

When word got out that Jacque had talked to the FBI, the other workers in chem ops were furious at her for endangering their high-wage jobs. She was harassed, cursed, and threatened both at the plant and in the community. After she was severely contaminated by a hole pierced into the glove that protected her from the plutonium she handled — "that's what you get for making waves," jeered a coworker — Jacque left her home, took her seven-year-old daughter out of school, and went into hiding.

Behind closed doors, a deal was struck between the US Justice Department and Rockwell International. Without any admission that the illegal incineration of plutonium had occurred, the Rocky Flats nuclear facility was eventually closed down and a cleanup arranged. However, the focus appeared to be more on cleaning up the evidence that implicated Rockwell International and the government than on decontaminating the land. The report of the grand jury, and the witness statements presented to it, were barred from public access. Jacque Brever's testimony, which she had risked her life to offer, was sealed away in a vault. The jurors who had considered the case were forbidden to talk about the evidence they'd seen.

With the full extent of the contamination covered up, the Department of Energy revealed its plans to turn the former Rocky Flats site into a wildlife refuge and recreational area where children might play. Wes McKinley, the foreman of the grand jury that had considered the case, was so appalled he decided to speak out:

> We heard much testimony, many documents, proving that this was one of the most contaminated places in the world and now we're going to let children come and roam freely, kick up the dust and breathe the plutonium scattered throughout there. We can't allow this to happen. If I speak out, I know I could go to prison. I'm willing to take that risk....For doing what I know to be right.[13]

Doing what is right for present and future generations may at times cause inconvenience for our families, jeopardize the career prospects of our colleagues, decrease profits for our employers, or even conflict with the law. Doing what feels right can leave us facing conflicting loyalties as well as opposition and intimidation.

When we are facing hard decisions, a question that can help orientate us is, "What happens through you?" Our decisions are like rudders that steer the flow not only of our lives but also of the unfolding stories we participate in. When Jacque Brever heard about

plans to create a recreational area on land contaminated with plutonium, she came out of hiding to add her voice to those campaigning
against this, saying: "After being part of the problem for so long, I
decided I wanted to be part of the solution."[14]

TRY THIS:
TELL ME, WHAT HAPPENS THROUGH YOU?

Repeat the process described on page 88, using the question, "What happens through you?"

OUR LARGER SELVES FEEL THROUGH US

Our emotions happen through us. But where do they come from?
If we see ourselves solely as separate individuals, then we think of
our feelings as arising within us and understandable purely in terms
of our own story. The approach of family therapy, based on understanding the family as a living system, takes a different view. A system is a whole that is more than the sum of its parts; what makes a
family more than just a collection of individuals is the way it functions as a whole. A family does this by feeling and acting through
its members.

When a family is functioning well, it rallies around and supports individual members through times of hardship. If there is a
crisis, such as a family member becoming seriously ill, the emotions
of alarm and concern will pass through the family, often transmitted
from one person to another, and activate a collective response. This
same process also happens with other human systems such as cohe-
sive teams or communities.

We can look at our pain for the world in a similar way: it is the
world system, or Gaia, feeling through us. The idea of being one

with all life might seem abstract or like an advanced spiritual state only attainable after many years of meditation. Yet when we're moved to tears by images of baby seals being clubbed to death, of the massacre of forests, or whichever wounds of our world hurt us most, we experience, directly, our interconnectedness with the living Earth.

DIFFERENT STORIES OF EVOLUTION

According to neo-Darwinists, evolution is a product of fierce competition, with each species pitted against the others in a vicious battle to survive. A quite different perspective now accepted by mainstream science is called *endosymbiotic theory*. This theory proposes that important steps in our evolution have occurred through cooperation between species, even to the point of separate organisms joining together to create entirely new forms of life. As its leading proponents, Lynn Margulis and Dorion Sagan, write, "Life did not take over the globe by combat, but by networking."[15]

If we trace the development of life from its earliest beginnings, we see a recurring pattern of smaller parts coming together to form larger integrated wholes. Initially there were only single-celled organisms. At some point in our evolutionary history came the remarkable transition from separate cells doing their own thing to organized groups of cells acting as single organisms. A further evolutionary jump came with the progression from simple multicelled organisms to complex forms of life containing different organs. Another major step came with the first social organisms, as insects like ants and bees formed complex communities that functioned as integrated systems. Human beings express this social tendency too, though at a higher level of complexity, which allows individuals to make their own choices while at the same time being part of a larger community.

Throughout human history we have followed this same evolutionary pattern of smaller parts coming together to form larger complex wholes. For hundreds of thousands of years, we existed as hunter-gatherers in small tribal groups highly responsive to changing conditions. With the development of agriculture, groups settled as larger village communities. Over time, villages joined together within clans or tribes, and these larger regional groupings formed alliances that became nations. Again and again peoples previously divided have made common cause and found a larger shared identity.

Crisis is one of the factors that can cause people to pull together. It can also have the opposite effect, triggering the collapse of communities and the unraveling of shared identities. With the planetary emergency we face, we are in danger of falling apart into factions fighting for what is left in a world we have depleted. Another possibility is that this crisis can become a turning point, the very danger moving us toward the next evolutionary leap.

THE EMERGENCE OF CONNECTED CONSCIOUSNESS

Something very interesting occurs when a group of jazz musicians improvise together. A number of separate individuals, all making their own decisions, act together as a whole. As the music flows, any of the musicians can take the solo spot, that leading role gliding seamlessly between the players. Who decides when the piano or trumpet player should come forward? It isn't just the person playing that instrument, for the others have already stepped back just a little to create an opening. There are two levels of thinking happening at the same time here; choices are made from moment to moment both by the group as a whole and by the individuals within it.

When people coordinate their actions through a collective thinking process, we can think of this as "distributed intelligence." No one person is in charge; the players act freely while being guided by their intention to serve the purpose of the group. For musicians to improvise together, they need to listen very attentively, expressing their individuality in a way that contributes to the overall sound. When they tune in to the group and become connected with it, it is as though the music itself plays through them.

A key feature of distributed intelligence is that no one part has to have the whole answer. Rather, the intelligence of the whole emerges through the actions and interactions of its parts. In a creative team, an idea may arise in conversation, then be added to and refined by other team members, its development shaped by everyone present. What allows a team to gel is a shift in identification, so that people identify with, and act for, the team rather than just themselves.

Could the next leap in evolution arise out of a shift in identification, in which we shed the story of battling for supremacy and move instead to playing our role as part of the larger team of life on Earth? Could the creativity and survival instinct of humanity as a whole, or even of life as a whole, act through us? Here connected consciousness stems from a widening of our self-interest, where we are guided by the intention to act for the well-being of all life. Within Buddhism, that intention is known as *bodhichitta*. Bodhichitta moves our focus from personal well-being to collective well-being.

We stand at an evolutionary crossroads, and we, collectively, could turn either way. Our own choices are part of that turning. We can choose, to borrow a phrase from *Star Trek*, the "prime directive" of our lives. When our central organizing priority becomes the well-being of all life, then what happens through us is the recovery of our world.

THE SHAMBHALA WARRIOR PROPHECY

A story that inspires us both is a twelve-centuries-old prophecy from the Tibetan Buddhist tradition. The heroes of this story are called Shambhala warriors. The term *Shambhala warrior* is a metaphor for the Buddhist figure of the bodhisattva, one who deeply understands the core teaching of the Lord Buddha. That central doctrine is the radical interdependence of all things. When taken seriously, this leads to the recognition that if one person has the capacity to be a bodhisattva, then all others do too.

Here is a particular version of the prophecy as it was given to Joanna by her dear friend and teacher Dugu Choegyal Rinpoche of the community of Tashi Jong in northwest India. Read it as if it were about you.

There comes a time when all life on Earth is in danger. At that time great powers have arisen, barbarian powers. And although they waste their wealth in preparations to annihilate one another, they have much in common. Among the things they have in common are weapons of unfathomable destructive power and technologies that lay waste to the world. It is just at this point in our history, when the future of all beings seems to hang by the frailest of threads, that the kingdom of Shambhala emerges.

You can't go there, because it is not a place. It exists in the hearts and minds of the Shambhala warriors. You can't tell whether someone is a Shambhala warrior just by looking at her or him, because these warriors wear no uniforms or insignia. They have no banners to identify whose side they're on, no barricades on which to climb to threaten the enemy or behind which to rest and regroup. They don't even have any home turf. The Shambhala warriors have only the terrain of the barbarian powers to move across and act on.

Now the time is coming when great courage is required of the Shambhala warriors — moral and physical courage. That is because they are going right into the heart of the barbarian powers to dismantle their weapons. They are going into the pits and citadels where the weapons are made and deployed, they are going into the corridors of power where the decisions are made. In this way they work to dismantle the weapons in every sense of the word.

The Shambhala warriors know these weapons can be dismantled because they are manomaya, which means "mind-made." They are made by the human mind and thus can be unmade by the human mind. The dangers facing us are not brought on us by some satanic deity or some evil extraterrestrial force, or by some unchangeable preordained fate. Rather, these dangers arise out of our relationships and habits, out of our priorities.

"So," said Choegyal, "now is the time for the Shambhala warriors to go into training." "How do they train?" Joanna asked. "They train in the use of two implements," he said. Actually, he used the term weapons. "What are they?" Joanna asked, and he held up his hands the way the dancers hold up the ritual objects in the great lama dances of his people. "One," he said, "is compassion. The other is insight into the radical interdependence of all phenomena."

You need both. You need compassion because it provides the fuel to move you out to where you need to be and to do what you need to do. It means not being afraid of the suffering of your world, and when you're not afraid of the world's pain, then nothing can stop you.

But by itself that implement is very hot; it can burn you out. So you need the other tool, the insight into the radical interconnectivity of all that is. When you have that, then you know that this is not a battle between the good guys and the bad guys. You know that the line between good and evil runs through the landscape of every human heart. And you know that we are so interwoven in the web of life that even our smallest acts have *repercussions that ripple through the whole web, beyond our ca-pacity to see. But that is kind of cool, even a little abstract. So you also need the heat of the compassion.*

That is the gist of the prophecy. If you've seen Tibetan monks chanting and making hand gestures, or mudras, most likely their hands are dancing the interplay between compassion and wisdom, which is there for each one of us to embody in our own way.

CHAPTER SIX

A Different Kind of Power

From our wider identity as part of the living Earth comes a strong urge to act. Yet while pain for the world alerts us to the urgency of our situation, we may still view planetary crisis as beyond our power to affect. In a recent large-scale survey, the Mental Health Foundation found that a feeling of powerlessness was, by far, the most common response to global issues.[1] Joe, a student blogging on the Web, expressed his experience of this:

> It seems to me that climate change is something only industrial and political leaders have any real power to solve. If we're honest, the idea that individuals like me can really contribute to a solution seems laughable. Am I wrong to think this way? Am I giving up?[2]

In seeing power as held only by those at the top of a hierarchy, Joe is expressing a view that is widespread and that undermines our capacity to act. When we see with new eyes, we discover a different way of perceiving and experiencing power. Before we move on to exploring this discovery, we need first to describe the old view of power and the problems it brings.

THE OLD VIEW OF POWER

In the old story, power is based on a position of dominance or advantage over others, a position that secures privileged access to resources and influence. This type of power is about getting your way and having others do what you want. The bottom line here is being able to win in a conflict; the more you can beat others, the higher you rise. We refer to this type of power as *power-over*. Let's see where it leads.

Feelings of Powerlessness Are Widespread

Power-over is based on a win-lose model; in the contest to come out on top, most of us end up losing. The position of being "in power" is such a small space that only a few people can fit there, leaving many feeling, as Joe the blogger expressed, that "the idea that individuals like me can really contribute to a solution seems laughable."

While we may be able to get our own way in some areas of our personal life, there is a limit to what we see as within our power. Because global issues are usually considered far beyond this, we may view thinking about them as a waste of time. For example, an expression we've often heard is "there's no point worrying about things you can't change, and you can't change the world."

Power Is Viewed as a Commodity

What gives a person a position of advantage over others? It is having something that others do not — whether it be money, weapons, material resources, contacts, or information. When information gives advantage, it becomes a tradable asset; as a result, valuable knowledge gets hidden away and public awareness is held back by secrecy.

Even votes in elections are thought of as buyable, with campaign·

funds dependent on huge donations from vested interest groups who expect favors in return. The power to shape the direction of our society has become a commodity to be bought and sold. When power is a possession to be held, defended, and accumulated, it becomes increasingly removed from the hands of ordinary people.

Power Generates Conflict

Power-over is essentially oppositional because gaining it involves taking it away from others. To rise up, either as an individual or as a group, you need to push others down; to get in power, you need to push others out. As those pushed down and out are left with resentment, those in power then need to keep tabs on the opposition and stop them from becoming powerful enough to present a threat.

Fear is intrinsic to this model of power. Even if and when you are on top, you have to be vigilant, lest you lose the upper hand. In the struggle to stay on top, ruthlessness and dishonesty have become so common that the link between power and corruption is often seen as inevitable.

Dominance gives privileged access to resources, and to maintain dominance, huge amounts are spent on being "strong," that is, able to win a fight. In 2010 the global arms expenditure was $1.6 trillion.[3] For perspective, spending 10 percent of this annually could eliminate extreme poverty and starvation throughout the world.[4]

Power Fosters Mental Rigidity

When displays of strength are seen as important, changing one's mind is viewed as "giving in," as a sign of weakness. In political discussions winning is valued more highly than deepening understanding. This standpoint blocks openness to new information and stifles the flexibility needed to deal with changing circumstances.

Power Becomes Suspect

When completing the sentence "Powerful people tend to be..." our workshop participants often reveal mixed feelings about becoming powerful, identifying both appealing and unappealing qualities. While they view powerful people as passionate, clear, determined, and brave, they also view them as more likely to be lonely, stabbed in the back, dishonest, and disliked.

This mixed picture presents a dilemma for those wanting to find the power to make a difference in the world but not wanting to enter a battleground where they are likely to become distrusted, lonely, or corrupted. Suspicion of power leads people to be reluctant to act authoritatively. Many have become disillusioned with mainstream politics: witness the low turnout at elections in many democracies. Fortunately, the power-over model isn't the only way to understand power. When we see with new eyes, a more attractive and capacity-building alternative comes into view.

A NEW STORY OF POWER

The word *power* comes from the Latin *possere*, meaning "to be able." The kind of power we will now focus on is not about dominating others but about being able to address the mess we're in. Rather than being based on how much stuff or status we have, this view of power is rooted in insights and practices, in strengths and relationships, in compassion and connection with the web of life.

One person who has embraced the collaborative model of power is Nelson Mandela. In the early 1980s, the apartheid government of South Africa had a highly trained army with advanced weaponry and nuclear missiles. Mandela, representing the African National Congress (ANC), had been in prison for more then twenty years. While many feared it might take a civil war to end it, apartheid didn't end because of victory in battle. Rather, the transformation came about through discussion and agreement. For that process to start, it needed, as Mandela put it, "jaw, jaw, jaw, not war, war, war." In his autobiography, *Long Walk to Freedom*, he describes coming to a decision to move this process forward while in solitary confinement:

> My solitude gave me a certain liberty, and I resolved to use it to do something I had been pondering for a long time: begin discussions with the government. This would be extremely sensitive. Both sides regarded discussions as a sign of weakness and betrayal. Neither would come to the table until the other made significant concessions.... Someone from our side needed to take the first step.[5]

When we respond to a situation in a way that promotes healing and transformation, we are expressing power. Mandela's contributions to establishing a multiracial democracy in South Africa offer a wonderfully inspiring example.

Because Mandela didn't have the authorization of the ANC's organizing committee, beginning talks with the enemy could have been seen as betrayal or as selling out. Taking this first step for peace took courage, determination, and foresight. Inner strengths like these are often thought of as things some people just have and others don't. These qualities, however, are linked to skills we can develop and practices we can learn. Thinking of courage and determination as things we *do* rather than things we *have* helps us to develop these qualities. They emerge out of our engagement with actual situations and the dynamics that arise from our interactions. This approach is relational, and we call it *power-with*.

1 + 1 = 2 AND A BIT

The discussions Mandela undertook were effective because both sides recognized that they stood to lose by going to war and that they would gain by finding a way to peace. They moved from a win-lose model of conflict to one aiming for a win-win outcome. The alternative to negotiations was likely to be a war in which both sides lost.

Power-with is based on *synergy*, where two or more parties working together bring results that would not have occurred if they had worked alone. Because something new and different emerges out of the interaction, we can think of it as "1 + 1 = 2 and a bit." This is another way of saying "the whole is more than the sum of the parts."

Emergence and synergy lie right at the heart of power-with. They generate new possibilities and capacities, adding a mystery element that means we can never be certain how a situation will go just from looking at the elements within it. We can know the strength of copper and of tin yet still be surprised by how much stronger bronze is, which comes from mixing the two together. The same thing can happen when we interact with others for a shared purpose. D. H. Lawrence wrote:

Water is H_2O,
Hydrogen two parts
Oxygen one
But there is also a third thing that makes it water
And nobody knows what that is.[6]

One place we can experience synergy is in conversation. If both sides have the courage and willingness to explore new ground, talking and listening to one another can open a creative space from which new possibilities emerge. That's what happened in the negotiations between Mandela and F. W. de Klerk, the South African president at the time. This unlikely duo jointly won the Nobel Peace Prize in 1993 for their extraordinary feat of navigating toward a peaceful settlement.

EMERGENCE

While the conversations between Mandela and de Klerk played a pivotal role in bringing apartheid to an end, this historic change wouldn't have happened without a much larger context of support. Within South Africa, people risked their lives daily to engage in the struggle for change. Around the world, millions of people played supporting roles by joining boycotts and campaigns. If we focus only on each separate activity, it is easy to dismiss it by thinking, "That won't do much." To see the power of a step, we need to ask, "What is it part of?" An action that might seem inconsequential by itself adds to and interacts with other actions in ways that contribute to a much bigger picture of change.

Remember our example of the newspaper photograph? When seen under a magnifying glass it appears as just a collection of tiny dots, but when, from a little distance, we see the photo as a whole, the larger pattern comes into view. In a similar fashion, a bigger picture of change emerges out of the many tiny dots of separate actions and choices. This link between small steps and big changes opens up our power in an entirely new way. Each individual step doesn't have to make a big impact on its own — because we can understand that the benefit of an action may not be visible at the level at which that action is taken.

Shared visions, values, and purposes flow through and between people. Nelson Mandela was deeply committed to a vision for his country that many were holding; the power of that vision moved through him and was transmitted to others. This type of power can't be hoarded or held back by prison walls; it is like a kind of electricity that lights us up inside and inspires those around us. When a vision moves through us, it becomes expressed in what we do, how we are, and what we say. The alignment of these three creates a whole that is more than the sum of its parts. The words below, from Mandela's defense at his trial in the 1960s, mean so much more because of the actions that followed them:

> During my lifetime I have dedicated myself to this struggle of the African people. I have fought against white domination and I have fought against black domination. I have cherished the ideal of a democratic and free society in which all persons live together in harmony and with equal opportunities. It is an ideal which I hope to live for and to achieve. But if needs be, it is an ideal for which I am prepared to die.[7]

The Power of Emergence

The concept of power-with contains hidden depths; so far we've described four aspects. First, there is the power of inner strengths drawn from us when we engage with challenges and rise to the occasion. Second, there is the power arising out of cooperation with others. Third, there is the subtle power of small steps whose impact only becomes evident when we step back and see the larger picture they contribute to. And last, there is the energizing power of an inspiring vision that moves through and strengthens us when we act for a purpose bigger than ourselves. All these are products of synergy and emergence; they come about when different elements interact to become a whole that is more than the sum of its parts.

At every level, from atoms and molecules to cells, organs, and organisms, complex wholes arise bringing new capacities into existence. At each level, the whole acts through its parts to achieve more than we could ever imagine from examining the parts alone.

So what new capacities emerge when groups of people act together to form larger complex social systems?

Our technologically advanced society has achieved wonders our ancestors could never have envisioned. We've put people on the moon, decoded DNA, and cured diseases. The problem is this collective level of power is also destroying our world. Countless seemingly innocent activities and choices are acting together to bring about the sixth mass extinction in our planet's history.

Seeing with new eyes, we recognize that we're not separate individuals in our own little bubbles but connected parts in a much larger story. A question that helps us develop this wider view is "What is happening through me?" Is the sixth mass extinction happening through us as a result of our habits, choices, and actions? By recognizing the ways we contribute to the unraveling of our world, we identify choice points at which we can turn toward its healing. The question "How could the Great Turning happen through me?" invites a different story to flow through us. This type of power happens through our choices, through what we say and do and are.

Not Needing to Know the Outcome

The concept of emergence is liberating because it frees us from the need to see the results of our actions. Many of our planet's problems, such as climate change, mass starvation, and habitat loss, are so much bigger than we are that it is easy to believe we are wasting our time trying to solve them. If we depend on seeing the positive results of our individual steps, we'll avoid challenges that seem beyond what we can visibly influence. Yet our actions take effect through such multiplicities of synergy that we can't trace their causal chain. Everything we do has ripples of influence extending far beyond what we can see.

When we face a problem, a single brain cell doesn't come up with a solution, though it can participate in one. The process of thinking happens at a level higher than just individual brain cells — it happens *through* them. Similarly, there's no way that we personally can fix the mess our world is in, but the process of healing and recovery at a planetary level can happen through us and through what we do. For this to happen, we need to play our part. That's where power-with comes in.

THE HELPING HAND OF GRACE

All the individuals on a team may each be brilliant by themselves, but if they don't shift their story from personal success to team success, their net effectiveness will be greatly reduced. When people experience themselves as part of a group with a shared purpose, team spirit flows through them, and their central organizing principle changes. The guiding question moves from "What can I gain?" to "What can I give?"

We can develop a similar team spirit with life. When we are guided by our willingness to find and play our part, we can feel as if we are acting not just alone but as part of a larger team of life that acts with us and through us. Since this team involves many other players, unsuspected allies can emerge at crucial moments; unseen helpers can remove obstacles we didn't even know were there. When we're guided by questions such as "What can I offer?" and "What can I give?" we might sometimes play the role of stepping out in front and at other times that of being the ally giving support. Either way, we think of the additional support behind our actions as a form of grace. Based on an interview with Joanna, this poem, edited into verse by Tom Atlee, founder of the Co-Intelligence Institute, expresses well the grace that comes from belonging to life:

> When you act on behalf
> of something greater than yourself,
> you begin

to feel it acting through you
with a power that is greater than your own.

This is grace.

Today, as we take risks
for the sake of something greater
than our separate, individual lives,
we are feeling graced
by other beings and by Earth itself.

Those with whom and on whose behalf we act
give us strength
and eloquence
and staying power
we didn't know we had.

We just need to practice knowing that
and remembering that we are sustained
by each other
in the web of life.
Our true power comes as a gift, like grace,
because in truth it is sustained by others.

If we practice drawing on the wisdom
and beauty
and strengths
of our fellow human beings
and our fellow species
we can go into any situation
and trust
that the courage and intelligence required
will be supplied.[8]

POWER-WITH IN ACTION

Here are three ways we can open to the kind of power we've been describing. We can:

- hear our call to action and choose to answer it.
- understand *power* as a verb.
- draw on the strengths of others.

Hear Our Call to Action and Choose to Answer It

There will be times when we become alerted to an issue and experience an inner call to respond. Choosing to respond to that call empowers us. Once we take that first step, we start on a journey presenting us with situations that increase our capacity to respond. Strengths such as courage, determination, and creativity are drawn forth from us most when we rise to the challenges that evoke them. When we share our cause with others, allies appear; synergy occurs. And when we act for causes larger than ourselves, the larger community for whom we do this will be acting through us.

We can experience our call to action in many different ways. Sometimes the uncomfortable discrepancy of realizing that our behavior is out of step with our values motivates us. Our conscience calls, and when we step into integrity, more of who we are heads in the same direction. At other times our call is more of a powerful summoning. We just know, even if we're not sure how, that we need to be somewhere, do something, or contact a particular person.

If we think of ourselves only as separate individuals, then we understand these intuitive calls purely in personal terms. Recognizing ourselves as part of the larger web of life leads to a different view. Just as we experience the Earth crying within us as pain for the world, we can experience the Earth thinking within us as a guiding impulse pulling us in a particular direction. We can view this as "co-intelligence," an ability to think and feel with our world.

Developing a sense of partnership with Earth involves listening for guiding signals and taking them seriously when we hear them. Our friend John Seed, the Australian rainforest activist, teaches a simple way of listening for such inner guidance. He calls it "a letter from Gaia," and it can be a powerful way of hearing our call to action.

TRY THIS: A LETTER FROM GAIA

If the Earth could speak to us, what would it say? We can take a step toward finding out by imagining the Earth can write through us.

On a blank sheet of paper, start a letter to ourselves that begins:

"Dear [insert your name]:

This is your mother Gaia writing…"

Continue the letter with whatever words come naturally, let your hand do the writing, don't think about it too much, and just let the words flow. If you would prefer to start this letter using different words, please do so.

Understand Power *as a Verb*

The old view of power is based on having more of something than the competing party. Power-with, however, is not a property or possession. It arises from what we *do* rather than what we *have*. The shift in perception from seeing power as a noun to seeing it as a verb has surprising potency. Here are two open sentences that invite an exploration of *power* as a verb.

TRY THIS:
OPEN SENTENCES THAT EMPOWER

These open sentences can be used in self-reflection or journaling or as a partnered listening exercise with someone
else.

1. I empower myself by...
2. What empowers me is...

When we have explored this exercise in workshops, people have
described empowering themselves by remembering what's important, doing what really matters, experiencing emotions, exercising
regularly, eating well, getting enough sleep, seeking out good company, meditating, paying attention to needs (their own and those of
others), laughing, dancing, and singing. When looking at what empowers them, participants have often mentioned inspiring purposes,
friends who encourage and support, and a sense of rootedness in
life. *Power* as verb points us in a very different direction from where
the noun form takes us.

Draw on the Strengths of Others

One way we can empower ourselves is by drawing on the strengths
of others. A wonderful example of this can be found in T. H.
White's *The Sword in the Stone*, when he tells the story of King
Arthur as a boy being tutored by Merlin.

The wizard Merlin, as Arthur's tutor, schooled the boy in wis-
dom by turning him into various creatures and had him live,
for brief periods, as a falcon, an ant, a wild goose, a badger,

a carp in the palace moat.... The time came when the new King of All England was to be chosen: it would be he who could draw the sword from the stone. All the famous knights, who came to the great tournament, went to the churchyard where the stone mysteriously stood, and tried mightily to yank out the sword that was embedded in it. Heaving and sweating, they competed to prove their superior strength. No deal; tug and curse as they might, the sword did not budge. When the disgruntled knights departed to return to their jousting, Arthur, who was just a teenager then, lingered behind, went up to the stone to try his own luck. Grasping the sword's handle he pulled with all his strength, until he was exhausted and drenched. The sword remained immobile. Glancing around, he saw in the shrubbery surrounding the churchyard the forms of those with whom he had lived and learned. There they were: badger, falcon, ant and the others. As he greeted them with his eyes, he opened again to the powers he had known in each of them — the industry, the cunning, the quick boldness, the perseverance...knowing they were with him, he turned back to the stone and, breathing easy, drew forth from it the sword, as smooth as a knife from butter.[9]

When we draw on a sense of fellowship, belonging, and connection, it is as if we are remembering our root system. This is power-with, which comes from the larger circle that we can draw on, that acts through us.

In his workshops, Chris sometimes asks people to remember a time when they did something that made a difference. It doesn't have to be anything grand, just something positive that might not have occurred otherwise. Then in groups of three or four, he asks people to take turns telling their stories and also identifying what strengths helped them play this role. After doing this, he often hears people say, "Hearing you describe using this strength helps me recognize it in myself too." When other people open to their strengths, it can help us open to ours too. We can "catch" this type of power from each other.

Whenever you are struggling, remember the sword in the stone. Think of trying to pull it out. Then pause. Remember those who inspire you. Think of them around you, and draw on their strengths. Think of those who support and believe in you. Draw strength from them as well. Think of who and what you are acting for, and feel their power acting through you too.

CHAPTER SEVEN

A Richer Experience of Community

There is an old folktale from Denmark about a meeting between two kings. "You see that tower," said the first king to the second, pointing to a tall, highly fortified part of his castle. "In my kingdom, I can command any of my subjects to climb to the top and then jump to their deaths. Such is my power that all will obey." The second king, who was visiting, looked around him and then pointed to a small, humble dwelling nearby. "In my kingdom," he said, "I can knock on the door of a house like that, and, in any town or village, I will be welcomed. Such is my power that I can stay overnight, sleeping well without any fear for my safety." The first king had power-over, and the second king had power-with. When we follow the path of partnership, a different quality of relationship emerges and, with this, a richer experience of community. In this chapter we'll look at fellowship and community as forms of wealth that enrich our lives, strengthen our security, and give us a more stable foundation from which to act.

THE EPIDEMIC OF LONELINESS

The term *community* is often used to describe those living in a specific location or having something in common such as a profession, activity, or ethnic background. But in modern urban environments, people can live in the same building yet still have no real connection to one another. Commenting on the widespread lack of social co-hesion in Western society, psychiatrist M. Scott Peck describes his experience of growing up in a New York apartment block:

> This building was the compact home for twenty-two fami-lies. I knew the last name of the family across the foyer. I never knew the first names of their children. I stepped foot in their apartment once in those seventeen years. I knew the last names of two other families in the building. I could not even address the remaining eighteen.[1]

The danger of being too comfortable, too self-sufficient, is that we lose any sense of needing one another. If each family has its own washing machine, electronic entertainment, and adequate sup-plies of food, what reason do we have to knock on our neighbors' doors? Experiencing need prompts people to reach out and make contact. That is why self-help groups like Alcoholics Anonymous have become such fertile expressions of community and fellow-ship. Through painful experience, their members have learned the truth of the maxim "I can't, we can." Crisis becomes a turning point when it provokes us to reach out to others.

Where do we look to meet our needs for security and a satisfy-ing life? In the story of Business as Usual, the central plot is about personal advancement through economic success; the assumption is that we meet our needs through getting more and better stuff. This story leads people to invest time, resources, and attention in their own little bubbles rather than in their relationships and com-munities. In the United States, for example, the proportion of peo-ple with no one to confide in has nearly tripled in recent decades.[2] While materially richer, on average, than they were thirty years ago (with an increase in billionaires as well as people living below the poverty line), modern Americans are less likely to visit friends or be visited by them.[3] Behind the locked doors lies an epidemic of loneliness that extends throughout the industrialized world.

Networks of mutual support bring many benefits, including reduced crime rates, higher levels of trust, lower suicide rates, a reduced risk of heart attacks, fewer strokes, and less depression.[4] Referred to as "social capital," the web of supportive relationships within a neighborhood is a form of wealth that improves the quality of our lives. Unfortunately, with the trend toward increased individualism and consumerism, this great treasure is in decline. The breakdown of communities is self-reinforcing: the more people retreat into their own private worlds, the more neighborhoods decline and the more people turn away from community involvement (see Fig. 7).

Figure 7. The vicious cycle of community erosion

A DIFFERENT WORLD IS POSSIBLE

Once in a while something occurs that sweeps away the isolation and mutual indifference so prevalent in modern society. Rebecca Solnit, in her book *A Paradise Built in Hell*, describes such a case:

I landed in Halifax, Nova Scotia, shortly after a big hurricane tore up the city in October of 2003. The man in charge of taking me around told me about the hurricane — not about the winds that roared at more than a hundred miles an hour and tore up trees, roofs, and telephone poles, or about the seas that rose nearly ten feet, but about the neighbors. He spoke of the few days when everything was disrupted, and he lit up with happiness as he did so. In his neighborhood all the people had come out of their houses to speak with each other, aid each other, improvise a community kitchen, make sure the elders were okay, and spend time together, no longer strangers.[5]

Our human tendency to pull together in emergency situations, even to risk our lives helping others, is well documented. In her study of human responses to disasters, Solnit describes how such rising to the occasion is more common than many suspect and more satisfying than many might imagine. Referring to her own experience of an earthquake in the San Francisco Bay Area in 1989, and the gratifying engagement she noticed in herself and others afterward, she writes:

> That sense of immersion in the moment and solidarity with others caused by the rupture in everyday life, an emotion graver than happiness but deeply positive. We don't even have a language for this emotion, in which the wonderful comes wrapped in the terrible, joy in sorrow, courage in fear. We cannot welcome disaster, but we can value the responses, both practical and psychological....Disasters provide an extraordinary window into social desire and possibility.[6]

When food appears reliably on our tables, we don't need to exercise our creativity or social intelligence to survive. It is different in a disaster. The closeness of danger activates our wits and our cooperative tendencies in ways that bring out new levels of aliveness and community. When the shops are flooded and the system is in disarray, the helping hand of a neighbor or an improvised soup kitchen offer more security than status or money. As we reach out to help one another, our lives become more meaningful and satisfying. We discover that we don't thrive, or survive, alone. That's what Helena Norberg-Hodge saw in the Ladakhi villagers of northern India (see chapter 5); knowing that their survival depended on the land and people around them, they experienced their interdependence as the very foundation of their reality.

What comes into view when we see with new eyes is this interdependence. There is no such thing as a "self-made man" or a "self-made woman": while we play a role in making ourselves, we are also made by each other and our world. When hurricanes, floods, and earthquakes sweep away illusions of self-sufficiency, we're reminded how much we need one another, how much we depend not only on people but also on the larger web of life. We treat people with a different kind of respect when we consider that they might someday be pulling us out of the rubble. We treat the rest of life with a different kind of respect when we consider that without it, we wouldn't be here at all.

Familiar Bubbles Beginning to Burst

We don't have to wait for a natural disaster before opening to the rich experience of community described by Solnit and others. We see this opening in our workshops on a regular basis. As participants express their grief, dread, and outrage at the unraveling of our world, awareness grows that we are, all of us, living in a disaster zone. Hearing one another name the tragedy unfolding in our world reassures us that we're not alone in noticing. The expression of common concern builds community, as does our shared willingness to show up and respond.

In our workshops we often use an exercise called "the milling" in which participants move around the room and then stop to face each other in pairs. We invite them to consider the possibility that the person in front of them might become a victim of the unraveling we face. With environmentally linked cancers, nuclear warheads still poised for action, and an increase in climate-related disasters, such a possibility is a sad reality. We then ask participants to consider the possibility that the person they face might make a crucial contribution to the healing of our world. This too is a realistic possibility.

This process drops the veil of normality that screens out the very real perils we face. The bubble of Business as Usual dissolves for a moment. This exercise also acknowledges that each of us can make a pivotal contribution to our world. We can never know whether our actions will have a decisive impact. What we can know is that by supporting one another, we make this possibility more likely.

At the moment, the impact of the unraveling is unevenly distributed. While climate-related disasters have wrecked the lives of millions of people, there are many millions more who, from the comfort of their homes, don't believe there is much of a problem.

As the unraveling of our world proceeds, it becomes more difficult to hide from. Unfortunately, shared awareness of a problem does not inevitably cause people to come together as a community of mutual support. When the danger is only vaguely sensed and not understood, this can lead to distrust, hostility, and scapegoating. In adversity, people can pull together or push apart, step outside their bubbles or retreat further into them.

The way we understand power greatly influences which way we go. The more people and nations apply a power-over model, the more they rely on force to maintain positions of advantage. This perspective fills the world with enemies against whom we must defend ourselves.

FOUR LEVELS OF COMMUNITY

The Shambhala warrior prophecy, recounted in chapter 5, describes a time of great danger where the hazards we face arise out of our relationships, habits, and priorities. The quest of the Shambhala warrior is to dismantle the mind-made weapons laying waste to our world.

The term *weapon* applies not only to armaments but also to destructive ways of thinking and acting. The pattern of thinking that divides humanity into us and them is something we can all play a role in dismantling. To do so, we use our two implements: compassion and insight into our interconnectivity with all life. These implements undo the thinking that creates enemies, leading us to community.

We can think of community as having different levels. Each progressively widens our sense of what we belong to, what we receive from, and what we act for. These levels are:

- groups we feel at home in
- the wider community around us
- the global community of humanity
- the Earth community of life

At each level, we can apply the implements of insight and compassion to dismantle the thinking that fragments our world and sets us against one another. The process of building community is self-reinforcing since not only does it contribute to the healing of our world, but it also enhances the quality of our lives. Like the second king in the Danish folktale, when we feel welcomed rather than threatened by those around us, we sleep more soundly at night. Let us look at each of these community levels in turn.

Groups We Feel at Home In

A group we feel at home in is small enough that we know one another's names and share common interests, even a common purpose. Feeling at home in such a group isn't always immediate; it can take time to build trust and a sense of ease. When we feel the bond of common cause and reciprocal support, we have a powerful setting for synergy.

We see this level of community at work in adventure stories in which a deeper purpose acts through a small group of central characters in a way that forges extraordinary loyalty between them. The bond among Harry, Hermione, and Ron in the Harry Potter stories grows out of their shared response to the grave danger they recognize. In *The Lord of the Rings*, Frodo acts with allies in the "fellowship of the ring" to accomplish their mission, and the lengths his friends go to for one another create a tough, enduring sense of community. The same can happen in our lives when we act with others toward shared goals.

A group we feel at home in can support us through remarkable personal transformations. Our interactions change when we feel safe enough to let go of defensiveness, allowing us to become more open to one another and to life. Ian, a colleague, described his experience in a group committed to supporting its members in offering their best contribution to the world:

> I had found a place where I could make a contribution simply by showing up, and showing care for those who also showed up. Slowly I found my voice in the group. I felt supported; it was like finding nourishing soil in which to grow.

A kind of magic can happen in groups like this. The fellowship generated anchors and nourishes us. As a lone voice, we can feel drowned out by the constant broadcast of commercial reality and swept along by the rush of Business as Usual. Circles of fellowship create space for a different story to be heard, spoken, and lived. By providing a protected space to share our concerns and sprout new responses, they serve as seedbeds for the Great Turning.

Seeing with new eyes involves recognizing a story much bigger than our personal dramas. Doing so fosters a different type of interpersonal economics, with more generosity and understanding. Issues such as who's getting the best deal or who has the most status fade in importance in comparison with what we can achieve together. Acting as a group for the Great Turning elevates our friendships and graces them with new beauty. Such groups powerfully support our ability to bring healing and transformation to our world. As anthropologist Margaret Mead so famously said:

> Never doubt that a small group of thoughtful, committed citizens can change the world. Indeed, it is the only thing that ever has.

We need groups like this now and will need them all the more in the coming years. They give us a foundation of resilience that helps us adapt to changing circumstances, recover from setbacks, and find strengths in times of adversity. When conditions are difficult, having a trusted gang around us both to draw from and give to can make all the difference. Doris Haddock, the activist fondly known as Granny D, was ninety-eight years old when she gave a talk in Philadelphia describing how this sort of mutual support transformed her experience of the Great Depression:

> Maybe we were hungry sometimes, but did we starve? No, because we had our friends and family and the earth to sustain us....We were fountains of creativity. We were fountains of friendship to our neighbors. As a nation, we were a mighty river of mutual support.[7]

The immediate circle in which we feel most at home is just the first rung of community. It is easy to build community with those who are like us and share our point of view. To dismantle the weapons laying waste to our world, however, we need to extend our community beyond this. We start with what is close and nourishing. But that is just the beginning.

The Wider Community around Us

In 1958 Dr. A. T. Ariyaratne was a young science teacher at a high school in Sri Lanka. In a remote poverty-stricken village, he organized a two-week work camp where he and his students helped the villagers identify pressing needs and work together in meeting them. The process of acting together and recognizing their own resources of strength and intelligence generated strong feelings of community. This initial effort eventually led to the emergence of a movement based on people working together to meet common needs. Called Sarvodaya Shramadana, a Sanskrit phrase meaning "the awakening of all through working together," this movement has spread across Sri Lanka to fifteen thousand villages.[8]

Sarvodaya applies the collaborative model of power-with, working on the principle that everyone can play a role and that everyone has something to offer. At community kitchens set up to tackle childhood malnutrition, all those present, including the children, are encouraged to contribute, even if they only bring some sticks for the fire. In offering their time, ideas, and energy, people grow respect for their own abilities and deepen their sense of community.

In one village, a water reservoir had needed repairing for more than fifteen years. The villagers had built up a thick file of their correspondence with local authorities requesting help. A work camp of local and visiting volunteers was organized by Sarvodaya to tackle the problem. The job was completed on the first day, and, at a celebration held in the village that evening, the file of letters was burned.

Sarvodaya challenges the view that our society's problems are beyond the power of ordinary people to address. By acting together, we make things possible that before had seemed impossible. Working collaboratively toward a common benefit can also be deeply satisfying because it transforms "work" into a social occasion. This principle was used to great effect with the barn raisings common in North America in the eighteenth and nineteenth centuries. It is applied today in a wealth of community-building projects around the world. The Transition movement, a global network of initiatives addressing community resilience, offers a good example.

As oil becomes less available and as fuel prices rise, the ensuing recession increases unemployment and financial stress. Eventually, we'll face an energy famine that threatens our industrial economy with collapse. If we don't have an alternative system in place to meet our basic needs, society is likely to break down into gangs fighting for food and other resources. The Transition movement focuses on developing strong and resilient communities that will be able to function when the oil age is over. For many communities around the world, the transition from oil dependence has already begun, and with it comes a renaissance of mutual aid.

A free booklet produced by Transition United States describes some simple initiatives that build community and save energy.[9] One is the "walking school bus" that has children walking to school in groups with one or more adults. This can be as informal as two or three families taking turns, or it can be more structured, with scheduled routes and trained volunteers. Another example is "permablitz," in which groups come together to transform one another's back- or front yards into gardens for growing food. Skills are shared, friends are made, and hard work is done with mutual enjoyment.

When viewed separately, initiatives like these might appear to have limited impact. Yet their power is revealed when we consider what they are part of and what they move toward. Each time people come together in acts of mutual aid, whether it be digging gardens or raising barns, they contribute to a new version of what our world can look like. The Great Turning involves changing our culture, and that means changing our neighborhoods as well.

The Global Community of Humanity

Martin Luther King Jr. was arrested in 1963 for taking part in a nonviolent civil rights protest in Birmingham, Alabama. From his prison cell, he wrote a famous letter responding to criticism of the demonstration and the role of "outsiders" in it:

> I am cognizant of the interrelatedness of all communities and states. I cannot sit idly by in Atlanta and not be concerned about what happens in Birmingham. Injustice anywhere is a threat to justice everywhere. We are caught in an inescapable network of mutuality, tied in a single garment of destiny. What affects one directly, affects all indirectly.[10]

"Outsider" involvement was criticized because of a belief that we should be concerned only with issues happening on our own doorsteps. Dr. King dismantled this assumption. We don't need to live geographically close to people in order to care about them or to take action on their behalf. What extends community is solidarity based on the two Shambhala warrior tools, compassion and insight into our interconnectedness. Distance does dull us, though. If children were starving outside our front door, it would be unnatural to ignore them. Yet throughout our world, ten children under the age of five die every minute because they don't have enough food to eat.[11]

To bring closer the realities of our deeply divided world, environmental scientist Donella Meadows calculated what a village of a thousand people would look like if it reflected the composition of the world's population.[12] The wealthiest two hundred people would receive three quarters of the village's income, while the poorest two hundred would receive just 2 percent between them. A third of the village would lack access to safe drinking water; of the 670 who were adults, half would be illiterate. Each year, there would be twenty-eight births and ten deaths, one of these from cancer, and three from lack of food or safe drinking water. Only half the married couples would have access to modern contraceptives.

In 2005 the statistics from this "state of the village report" were updated, though they showed no improvement in the striking inequalities described fifteen years earlier in the first edition.[13] Our world village faces the pattern of overshoot and collapse looked at in chapter 1. Because freshwater is being extracted at a rate faster than it is replenished, wells around the village are drying up. Because the land is overfarmed and topsoil is being lost to erosion, the area of productive agricultural land is shrinking. Because of overfishing, stocks of many once-common species have either collapsed or are in sharp decline. Even without taking climate change into account, it is easy to see that we are heading for a crash.

If we lived in this village, would we see where we were headed? Would we pull together to address the challenges we face? Unfortunately, as reflected by our current global situation, the village would be divided into groups that see themselves as separate from, and in competition with, one another. A large share of the village wealth would be spent on military operations to keep resources in the hands of the richer groups within the village, some of whom would be in conflict with each other. As these resources became depleted, wars would be waged over remaining reserves.

Thinking back to the two Danish kings, we see that sending young people to death and dismemberment in war is not so different from ordering them to jump from a tall, fortified tower. In contrast, the Great Turning is about creating the sort of global community where people are able to sleep at night without fear for their safety.

When Helena Norberg-Hodge first visited Ladakh in 1975, she was told by one of the villagers, "We don't have any poor people here."[14] She saw he was speaking the truth: everyone's basic needs certainly appeared well met. There were no very rich people either — not in a material way, at least. In terms of social capital, though, the Ladhakhi were among the wealthiest people she had ever known, and the happiest. They would sing together while bringing in the harvest. Their peacefulness was infectious. A phrase she kept hearing the villagers say was "we have to live together."[15] When a conflict arose, they would repeat this like a mantra and find a way of getting on. What would it be like if this were our mantra too?

We can choose between different types of wealth. The path of seeking material wealth beyond our basic needs sets us against one another. The greater a nation's appetite for resources, the more likely it is that it will go to war, and the more likely it is to tear up forests for open strip mines or to drill for oil deep below the ocean floor, wrecking marine habitats. The second type of wealth is what we see with new eyes. It is the community we find in mutual belonging.

The Earth Community of Life

Because she loved a river, Ali Howard swam almost 380 miles in twenty-eight days.[16] The rich ecosystems of the Skeena in Canada are threatened by Shell's plans to drill a thousand gas wells around the headwaters of this river. As the small, scattered gas deposits are buried within seams of coal, high-pressure water and chemicals would be pumped into the ground as part of the extraction process. The contaminated silt washed into local streams would threaten the spawning grounds of salmon not just in the Skeena but also in the nearby Nass and Stikine rivers too. To draw attention to the devastation these gas wells would bring, Ali swam the full length of the Skeena. Along her route, those living by the river came out to greet her, joining together in a newfound watershed identity.

Communities don't just involve humans; they include all that we belong to, feel part of, identify with, and act for. For Ali Howard, her community included the River Skeena itself and the rich ecology of plants, animals, and people within its watershed. When we stand up for a community, it is as though the community acts and speaks through us, making us its mouthpiece. Ali gave the Skeena someone to speak through.

This role, of speaking for our natural world, is crucial. If we don't, who will? Unless someone speaks for the salmon, the rivers, the wild spaces, and the rest of life, how will we stop the relentless drive of short-term profiteering that is turning our world into a wasteland? Our survival is at stake; we are only beginning to realize how ecosystems act together to maintain conditions favorable to humans. As James Lovelock, the leading scientist behind Gaia theory explains, "The natural world outside our farms and cities is not there as decoration but serves to regulate the chemistry and climate of the Earth, and the ecosystems are the organs of Gaia that enable her to maintain our habitable planet."[17]

An understanding of our interdependence with all life is found in the wisdom of many indigenous cultures. As the Mohawk Thanksgiving Prayer states, "we have been given the duty to live in balance and harmony with each other and all living things."[18]

This duty is based on the recognition that without the interconnected web of ecosystems, we have no life. Yet we humans are living as if we were at war with the rest of nature, eliminating whole ecosystems and driving entire species to extinction. Of the species assessed in 2009 by the International Union for the Conservation of Nature (IUCN), 17,921 were deemed to be at serious risk of extinction.[19] We just don't know what impact the loss of these species would have, but activist and writer Duane Elgin offers a metaphor:

> Our extermination of other species has been compared to popping rivets out of the wings of an airplane in flight. How many rivets can the plane lose before it begins to fall apart catastrophically? How many species can our planet lose before we cross a critical threshold where the integrity of the web of life is so compromised that it begins to come apart, like an airplane that loses too many rivets and disintegrates?[20]

"We need to live together," the Ladhakhi villagers say. "Or we will not live at all" is the message modern biologists would add. To stop the extinctions, we need to declare peace with our world. For that peace to take root and grow, we need active reconciliation and community building.

In the mid-1980s, Joanna and John Seed developed a group process that strengthens our felt relationship with other life-forms. Called the Council of All Beings, it invites us to step aside from our human identity and speak on behalf of another form of life.[21] It can be an animal, a plant, or a feature of the environment — an otter, an ant, a redwood, or a mountain. We represent these life-forms at a gathering of beings who meet in council to report on the condition of our world. On one level we can see this as an improvised group drama, where we build empathy by looking through the eyes of another party. We could also approach this as a spiritual process, as a ritual inviting a shift in consciousness that allows another part of our world to speak through us. Either way, we are dropping our normal lenses and taking a perspective that sensitizes us to the needs and rights of other beings.

In preparation, we take time "to be chosen" by the life-form we will represent. Then, in silence, we make masks. At the appointed time, often announced with the beat of a drum, we join together in a circle and listen as each being speaks in turn.

When we speak on behalf of another life-form, a shift happens in our relationship with it. If we have spoken for ants or glaciers, bringing our imagination to bear in reporting their experience, they are no longer strangers to us. What emerges is a deepened appreciation of how they are affected by human activity, and with this, a sense of solidarity with them and a desire that they be well.

Like Arthur drawing on the strengths of creatures Merlin had sent him to spend time with, we can experience the beings we speak for as sources of support. Here Chris describes a time when this happened for him:

> *I was going through a difficult patch and sat down by a tree. I looked up and recognized the dark buds. It was Ash. I had been Ash and felt a sense of reunion with an old friend. Looking down, I saw Ivy. I had been Ivy too, at a different Council of All Beings. I felt supported by these two plants; I had a relationship with them I felt comforted by. My experiences of these councils have had a profound impact on my relationship with the life-forms I have represented. They have become significant as allies in my life. I wish to be an ally to them too.*

This is the fourth dimension of community, in which we feel welcomed by our world and supported by it. Feeling part of a much larger team can anchor and steady us through times of difficulty. When we have this "team spirit," we feel a heightened sense of spiritual connection with life.

CHAPTER EIGHT

A Larger View of Time

In the largest fraud of its kind in history, Bernard Madoff swindled his victims out of more than $20 billion. For years, he maintained an illusion of profitability by siphoning capital from investments to pay his customers a return. In the long term, a Ponzi scheme like this is bound to collapse; the resource base of investments gets used up, and sooner or later there is not enough money left to pay people back. But until that point is reached and the fraud exposed, it seems a good bet. While Madoff's actions were illegal, the practice of making quick bucks by plundering a resource that people depend on is not. Mainstream economics makes such short-term profiteering lucrative, even though it inevitably generates tragedies for the future. The problem is that costs are only counted if they appear in a very short window of time. The sorry tale of our oceans' fisheries provides a good example.

For hundreds of years, fishing communities along the coast of Newfoundland thrived, thanks to plentiful supplies of cod. From the 1960s onward, the use of larger ships equipped with sonar, on-board refrigeration, and much larger nets led to a massive increase in the catch. The cost of this, not counted at the time, was the almost complete elimination of the northwest Atlantic cod population (see Fig. 8.1, which shows the annual cod catch off the east coast of Newfoundland over a period of 150 years).[1] The same pattern of industrial-scale fishing has led to widespread collapse of fish stocks around the world. Once common species, such as the Atlantic blue-fin tuna and the common skate, are now threatened with extinction. If current trends continue, scientists predict that by the middle of this century commercial sea fishing could come to an end.[2]

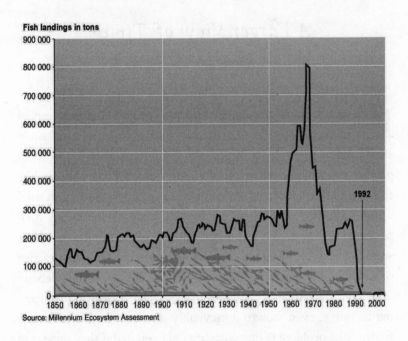

Figure 8.1. Growth in the fishing industry followed by overshoot and collapse

Alan Greenspan, former chief of the US Federal Reserve, describes short-term thinking that ignores future costs as "under-pricing risk," calling it a fundamental cause of the financial crisis.[3] His view is that our blindness to longer-term risks is a feature of human nature and, as a result, we're doomed to repeat the same mistakes. But is it human nature or the product of a peculiar way of perceiving time that has, unfortunately, become mainstream in the industrial world?

When the Haudenosaunee meet in council to consider major

decisions, their practice is to ask, "How will this affect the seventh generation?" This chapter describes how we too can live within a larger view of time. We will explore the concept of "deep time" and look at how it not only promotes greater ecological intelligence but also opens up new sources of strength, inspiration, and support.

A Family View of Time

When New College at Oxford University was founded in 1379, huge oak timbers were used to hold up the roof of its great dining hall. To provide replacement timbers for the roof's eventual repair, the college foresters planted a grove of oaks on college land. Since the beams were two feet wide and forty-five feet long, it would take several hundred years for the trees to grow to the size required. The foresters were thinking ahead in a time frame of centuries.

York Minster Cathedral in England took more than two hundred and fifty years to build, while the temple complex of Angkor Wat in Cambodia was constructed over more than four centuries. The Neolithic structure at Stonehenge, with stones weighing four tons each that were transported from 240 miles away, is thought to have taken fifteen hundred years to complete. The craftspeople, architects, and planners in these projects must have accepted the fact that the work to which they were giving themselves would not be completed within their lifetimes, or even within the lifetimes of their children.

Closer to home, a widened view of time is also found in the way most people think about their families. Families extend backward in time, and all over the world significance is given to lineage, ancestry, and family trees. When looking back at our family roots, at any point in history there will be a familiar constellation of parents, brothers, sisters, grandparents, aunts, uncles, cousins, children, and grandchildren. Over time, individual characters arrive, play their part, move through different roles, and then die; the larger system of the family, meanwhile, lives on.

When we see ourselves as part of a family system like this, we locate ourselves in a story that spans centuries. In each historical period there is the same enduring motivation to care for the next generation, as the extended family acts through its members to keep itself alive. Hamish, a father of two young children, described his experience of this family mode of time by saying:

I'm part of a family that is six foot tall,
several yards wide,
and hundreds of years long.

Families, of course, extend forward as well. In addition to our roots, there are shoots still growing and branches that will sprout from them. If seeing ourselves as part of a family is an important aspect of our identity, then for how long would we like our family to continue? If the next generation matters to us, and the children born to it do as well, then what about their children, and their children's children? Is there a point in time when we draw a line that says beyond this they no longer count?

This question may sound ridiculous, but unfortunately the line drawn in corporate and governmental decision-making is frighteningly close. There is a time horizon beyond which consequences cease to be accounted for or even considered. Much of government planning works within a time frame of just a few years. When the long term is considered, the period looked at rarely stretches beyond a few decades. In major financial institutions, where the price difference between the morning and the afternoon can lead to profit or loss, even a few months into the future can seem farther ahead than is worth considering. Such extreme short-term thinking is a fairly recent phenomenon and is linked to an acceleration in our experience of time.

TIME IS SPEEDING UP

In agricultural societies, the year's rhythm is counted in seasons. In the days before clocks, the sun moving across the sky gave shape to the day. Compare these natural cycles with the time intervals of modern technology, now measured in fractions of a microsecond. Life has become a race in a way that is historically unprecedented.

The sense of hurry is spurred on by an economic system that sets its goals and measures its success in terms of how fast it is growing. For an economy to grow from one year to the next, more needs to be accomplished in the same amount of time. If we want growth every year, then our speed of activity has to constantly increase.

Computer technology makes it possible to measure how fast companies are growing and to instantly compare vast numbers of them with each other. This has sped up the process of buying and selling company stock. In 1998 the average stock ownership period was two years. With the increased use of software-controlled automatic trading, stocks may now be held only for days, weeks, or months.[4] Much of this buying and selling is done by investment funds. Since the bonuses of fund managers are linked to how fast their funds are growing, they increasingly use their shareholder influence to push for maximum short-term returns. Company costs are cut through shedding staff, relying on casual or cheaper overseas labor, and neglecting maintenance. The constant pressure to improve returns leads employees to feel increasingly driven. Defending this approach, the managing partner of one of the world's leading private equity firms said:

> A lot of public companies we speak to spent too much time on regulatory issues, social responsibility and corporate

governance....And they forget their prime purpose — which
is to grow the company as rapidly as possible.[5]

THE COST OF SPEED

The experience of speed can be pleasurable. There is a thrill to
whizzing down a hill, an ease in instantly accessing information, and
a joy to moving through tasks rapidly. When so much needs to be
done to address our planetary crisis, speed is necessary. At the same
time, there is a big difference between choosing to go faster when
doing so genuinely brings benefit and being caught in a pattern of
hurry through habit or demand. Because the valuing of speed is so
embedded within our society, most people end up feeling so rushed
and so short of time that their life becomes one long race.

Chronic hurry exacts a heavy toll. Straining against time affects
our bodies, with release of adrenaline, tightening of muscles, and acceleration of the heart. While short bursts of pressure can be good for
us, chronic stress wears us down, increasing our risk of heart disease,
infections, depression, and many other conditions. Our relationships
suffer too. A common factor in marital and family breakdown is a
shortage of time to connect. In the long term, a sprint cannot be sustained, and burnout reduces performance. Crashing into a problem is
often the wake-up call that alerts people to the hazards of high-speed
living. If learned from, crisis can become a turning point. The key to
recovery, as we shall see, is a larger view of time.

When we are overwhelmed by numerous short-term goals and
targets, we lack enough time and space to consider what lies over
the horizon. Rushing narrows our field of vision to the immediate
moment. The past becomes irrelevant and the future abstract. Such
narrow timescapes lead to the following five problems:

- Short-term benefits outweigh long-term costs.
- We don't see disasters coming our way.

- Narrow timescapes are self-reinforcing.
- We export problems to the future.
- Narrow timescapes diminish the meaning and purpose of our lives.

Let us examine each of these problems in turn.

Short-Term Benefits Outweigh Long-Term Costs

The classic example of short-term benefits outweighing long-term costs is addictive behavior, where the allure of a cigarette, a drink, or a line of cocaine is its immediate effect. The downside of a behavior fails to deter us if it falls outside the bubble of time to which we give our attention. The same dynamic applies to dishonesty, which might seem a quick way out of a fix but has delayed effects that are toxic to relationships and decision making. The issue of unsustainability arises from a similar narrowing of timescape. As the example of the fishing industry so clearly illustrates, the pursuit of continual growth in a resource-constrained world is a recipe for disaster.

We Don't See Disasters Coming Our Way

When we travel at great speed but only look a short distance into the future, disasters appear to come out of the blue. The story of the *Titanic* offers an important teaching. Several days before the sinking, the captain had received warnings about icebergs over the radio. He had changed course slightly but not slowed down. On the evening of the crash, two ships had radioed warnings of icebergs, but the radio operator was snowed under with a backlog of personal messages and hadn't passed the warnings on. "Shut up, shut up, I'm busy," he'd replied when called at 11:00 p.m. by a nearby ship surrounded by ice. Forty minutes later, lookouts spotted a large iceberg straight in front. By then, the momentum of such a large ship traveling at close to full speed allowed no time for a change in course. Thirty-seven seconds later, the iceberg struck its fatal blow.

While there is always uncertainty when assessing future risks, some problems are reasonably foreseeable; they are like icebergs that our industrial society is racing toward. When we view these problems as farther down the road in time, we treat them as non-urgent and leave them to one side. It is well-known that oil reserves are limited and in decline, yet there is great resistance to any slowing down of our oil-dependent economy. We would need the resources of another three to five planets like Earth if everyone lived the lifestyle of the average Westerner, yet the consumer lifestyle is still aggressively promoted throughout the world. Business as Usual can only proceed if we close our eyes to where it is taking us.

Narrow Timescapes Are Self-Reinforcing

Living in a shrunken bubble of time is similar to being agoraphobic in that it is self-reinforcing. People don't want to look too far into the future because doing so can bring up despair and guilt. Retreating into the "home" of a familiar timescape brings short-term relief but also undermines the motivation to act for our world; this adds to the feeling that we are culpable. The way out of this trap is to recognize the important function guilt can serve and to honor this emotion as an expression of our pain for the world. Guilt is the uncomfortable awareness that our actions are out of step with our values. If we, collectively, don't experience guilt for what we're inflicting on future generations, we are in danger of pulling a "Madoff" on them. The beautiful world we were entrusted to protect will have been all used up.

We Export Problems to the Future

Our industrial economy is based on the practice of externalizing costs. This makes goods and services cheaper for those living now but leaves behind a debt incurred by us but not paid for. A common example is when a company reduces its budget for safety and maintenance. This increases the risk of accidents, but because risk refers to events that haven't happened yet, they don't appear on the balance sheet. They are a cost that is projected forward in time.

When the *Exxon Valdez* oil tanker crashed in 1989, releasing oil that contaminated more than a thousand miles of Alaska's shoreline, the radar was switched off because it had been broken for a year and not repaired. Just ten months before this, oil company executives at a top-level meeting in Arizona had been warned that safety equipment was inadequate. The executives chose to save money rather than to address the problem.[6] Twenty-one years later, more than four million barrels of oil poured into the Gulf of Mexico from BP's Macondo well. The presidential commission investigating this catastrophe found a similar pattern of cost-cutting on safety, reporting that "many of the decisions that BP, Halliburton, and Transocean made that increased the risk of the Macondo blowout clearly saved those companies significant time (and money)."[7]

These disasters are not isolated events: between 1996 and 2009, there were seventy-nine major spills from oil and gas drilling in the Gulf of Mexico, with the presidential commission finding an industry culture of complacency.[8] Fossil fuels and the things we use them for are artificially cheap because we don't count the costs we're passing on to future generations. Climate change is another example: with the world warming up, the ice sheets of Greenland and West Antarctica are already melting. The water these store can raise sea levels by forty feet, which would cause flooding in two-thirds of the world's major cities.[9] While this might happen over an extended period of time, the images of New Orleans under water after Hurricane Katrina give a glimpse of what we are setting in motion.

Among our greatest crimes against future generations is the production of radioactive waste; through its mutagenic impact on the gene pool, its harmful effects are permanent. Because radioactivity is invisible, it will be difficult for future generations to know where the danger lies, so they won't be able to protect themselves. The shore of Lake Karachay in the Chelyabinsk province of Russia doesn't look hazardous, but it is so contaminated that a lethal dose of radiation can be received just by standing there for an hour.[10]

In the early 1950s, the lake was a depository for waste from the Mayak nuclear complex. Then, in 1957, at a nearby storage facility, the Kyshtym disaster occurred. A long-kept secret, this is one of the world's worst nuclear accidents. A fault in the cooling system of an underground storage tank led to an explosion that threw off the 160-ton concrete lid and blew seventy tons of highly radioactive fission products into the atmosphere. A dust cloud spread radioactive isotopes over nine thousand square miles, contaminating 270,000 Soviet citizens and their food supplies.

Each year, another twelve thousand tons of high-level waste are produced by the world's nuclear reactors. This waste contains isotopes that include Iodine-129 (with a half-life of more than 15 million years), Plutonium-239 (with a half-life of 24,000 years, but which decays into Uranium-235, with a half-life of 700 million years) and Neptunium-237 (with a half-life of more than 2 million years). We don't have a long-term solution for the safe disposal of nuclear waste. We don't know how to make containers that can withstand the embrittling effect of their radioactive contents. Much of the most toxic waste is kept in steel and concrete casks designed for a lifespan of a hundred years at best. We don't have a clear plan for what to do after this. It is a problem, and a cost, we are passing forward in time. As the fate of nuclear power stations built on earthquake fault lines in Japan so tragically illustrates, we are creating disasters that are waiting to happen, with harmful consequences that continue virtually forever.

Narrow Timescapes Diminish the Meaning
and Purpose of Our Lives

Within the story of Business as Usual, a million years in the future, or even a thousand, is completely off the screen. When we are under time pressure, even ten years ahead might seem too distant to pay attention to. Dashing from one thing to another, we lose sight of where we're going. When life is dominated by urgent demands, we don't get the time needed to find our direction or determine what really matters. We can spend our days being busy without having our heart in what we do. This kind of busyness takes us further away from what's most important to us.

Thinking only in short stretches of time also severely limits our sense of what can be achieved through us. To grow a project fruitful enough to be inspiring takes time. It is easy to ask, "What's the point?" if we're not seeing results after six months or a year. Imagine what would happen if we applied the same thinking after planting a tender young date palm or olive tree. These trees can take decades to become fully productive, but once they do they remain so for more than a century. When we move beyond thoughts of individual achievement and consider what our actions, when combined with the actions of others, can bring about, we open to a more gripping story.

TRAVELING IN TIME

In 1988 Joanna invited a dozen friends to join her in a study-action group on radioactive waste. During the previous years, she had asked scientists, engineers, and activists what they thought could be done with our nuclear facilities and materials once they were no longer in use. When she visited the construction site of a deep geological repository in New Mexico, the manager proudly told her about the high-tech barriers and signage that could deter intruders for a hundred years. "And after that?" Joanna had asked. He looked baffled. Larger time spans were outside his frame of reference, as they were for others with whom she spoke. That is why she had invited the dozen friends. She wanted to create a space to explore human responsibilities grounded in a larger view of time.

The group took turns researching and presenting topics. One November day it was Joanna's turn, and the information she had gathered, about US nuclear waste containment practices, was both technical and horrific. To sustain attention and motivation, she needed some help. It came from an unusual direction.

On the door, Joanna put up a sign reading CHERNOBYL TIME LAB: 2088. As people came in, a recording of Russian liturgical music set the tone. Initiating their first group experience of traveling through time, she said:

> Welcome! Our work here at the time laboratory of this Guardian Site is based on the importance of being able to journey backward through time. This is because the decisions made by people in the late twentieth century on how to deal with the poison fire (or radioactivity, as they called it then) have such long-term effects. We must help them make the right decisions. So you have been selected to go back in time to a particular group in Berkeley, California, that has come to our attention. They are meeting exactly one hundred years ago today to try to understand, with their limited mentality, the ways their "experts" are containing the poison fire. It is easy for this group to feel ignorant and discouraged. Therefore, we will go backward in time to enter their bodies as they proceed with their study so that they will not become disheartened.
>
> Our research reveals that in time travel an essential factor is intention — strong, unwavering belief in the purposes the heart has chosen. If our intention is clear, we can travel back

a century to enter the hearts and minds of this very group. It will take about thirty seconds.

Joanna turned up the music for half a minute, then, switching it off, simply proceeded to present the day's topic. In the course of the session, no one commented on its odd beginning. Everyone was too keenly focused on the material itself. But there was a sense of heightened caring in the room, as though everyone had an added internal presence that was encouraging and supportive. By opening the group's imagination to the possibility that future beings can help us face the mess we are in, she helped the group discover a welcome source of additional inspiration. The use of imaginary time travel, often sparked or accompanied by music, has since become a regular feature of the Work That Reconnects. It offers rich and rewarding opportunities to widen the timescape we inhabit and to draw on the support of past and future beings.

ANCESTORS AS ALLIES

For much of the world's population, it is not so strange to think that those living elsewhere in time might be able to help us. Shrines to ancestors are common in Japan and Korea, and the practice of seeking guidance from those who have lived before us is an accepted part of many indigenous traditions. As West African shaman and author Malidoma Somé writes:

> In many non-Western cultures, the ancestors have an intimate and absolutely vital connection with the world of the living. They are always available to guide, to teach and to nurture.[11]

The interest ancestors take in us is a natural extension of the care parents have for their children, or grandparents for their grandchildren. When we're struggling or feeling alone, we can find moral strength in opening to a sense of ancestral support. Just as an athlete may perform better when cheered by a crowd, we can imagine a crowd of ancestors cheering us on in all that we do to ensure the flow of life continues.

If the role of the ancestors is to look out for those following them in time, then it follows that we too play this role. Those living in the future will look back on us as their ancestors. Recognizing future beings as our kin brings them closer to us. Within the narrow timescape of Business as Usual, they are a forgotten people whose interests have disappeared from view. When we recognize that we are their ancestors, a sense of care and responsibility arises naturally.

Connectedness with ancestors and with future generations lifts us out of the microplots of Business as Usual and places us in a truer and more expansive story. In life's epic journey, every one of our ancestors lived long enough to pass on the spark of life. This ancestry extends back in time far beyond the reaches of our human past. With the shift in identity to our ecological self, we discover that the entire span of recorded history is just a fraction of a page in a more extensive volume.

OUR JOURNEY AS LIFE ON EARTH

We belong to a planet four and a half billion years old. To make relative time periods easier to grasp, let us look at the entire history of our Earth as a single twenty-four-hour day starting at midnight.[12] In this day of planet-time, each minute would mark the passing of more than three million years (see Fig. 8.2).

At first, the planet was as hot as an erupting volcano. Being formed by the gravitational pulling together of materials orbiting the sun, it was continually showered by meteorites. Shortly after midnight, a chunk of matter the size of a small planet had collided with Earth, the impact causing materials to be thrown outward into space to form the moon. It took till nearly two in the morning for the planet surface to cool down enough for steam in the atmosphere to condense into rainfall. As rain fell and kept falling, the oceans were born.

Between three and four in the morning, the first forms of life appeared in warm, shallow water. There were only traces of oxygen in the atmosphere and no ozone layer to provide protection from incoming ultraviolet radiation, which was too strong to allow life to develop on land. It took till ten-thirty in the morning for photosynthesis to evolve, and from then on, those early green life-forms started producing oxygen as a waste product.

All life-forms were single celled and remained so for the rest of the day, the first more complex multicelled organisms not evolving till half past six in the evening. By eight, worms had appeared at the bottom of shallow seas, followed an hour and twenty minutes later by the first fish. By a quarter to ten, plant life had become established on land; soon after ten, amphibians and then insects appeared.

At twenty to eleven, disaster struck in what has been described as the mother of all mass extinction events. A combination of volcanic activity, asteroid impacts, and other disasters wiped out 95 percent of life, though that left plenty of room for the dinosaurs to emerge afterward as the dominant vertebrates on land. The age of the dinosaurs lasted till twenty to midnight, when a six-mile-wide meteorite struck earth and caused a dust cloud to block out so much sunlight that the decline in plant life killed off many large animals. Mammals, who had been quietly in the background for the last hour, emerged to fill the niche of dominant vertebrates on land. Ten minutes later, some mammals returned to the sea and slowly evolved into whales and dolphins.

At two minutes to midnight, a small ape in Africa became the last common ancestor of both humans and chimpanzees. At just twenty seconds to midnight, apelike hominids discovered the use of fire. The entire history of our species, from its early origins in Africa, is contained in the last five seconds before midnight.

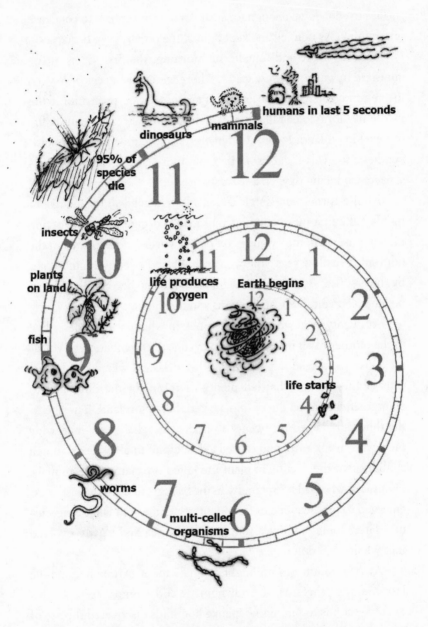

Figure 8.2. Four and a half billion years of our planetary history represented as a single day. Each hour represents 187.5 million years. Each minute represents 3.125 million years.

Within the story of Business as Usual, a commonplace saying is "you can't change human nature." But when we look at the breathtaking span of our planetary history, the idea that "we'll never change" seems absurd. We are part of the most extraordinary unfolding. Where will it go next?

OUR JOURNEY AS A SPECIES

To get a clearer sense of the critical point in human history we have reached, we can take that last five seconds of the planet's day and represent it as a twenty-four-hour time period (see Fig. 8.3). We are moving from planet-time to human time, where all our history is represented by a single day.[13]

While apelike relatives using stone tools and fire had been around a million years ago, our species, Homo sapiens, is thought to be a quarter of a million years old. If we take the past 240,000 years as our day, and represent each ten thousand years by an hour, we didn't leave Africa till six in the evening. For 95 percent of our history, we lived in small groups as hunter-gatherers (as some indigenous people still do today), only turning to agriculture at ten to eleven in the evening. A few minutes later, the first recorded city, Jericho, arose.

By twenty past eleven at night, we'd discovered the wheel and were beginning to develop early forms of writing. By half past eleven, work on Stonehenge had begun, and the first city-states were developing in Egypt, China, Peru, Iran, the Indus Valley, and the Aegean. At a quarter to midnight, the Buddha and Confucius were both alive, with Jesus coming a few minutes later and Muhammad a few minutes after that.

At five minutes to midnight, windmills were in use, and two minutes later, Christopher Columbus reached North America. In this full day representing human history, the industrial age didn't begin till two minutes before midnight. In the last minute, the world population rose from just over a billion to seven billion. In the last twenty seconds (that is, since 1950), we have used up more resources and fuel than in all human history before this.

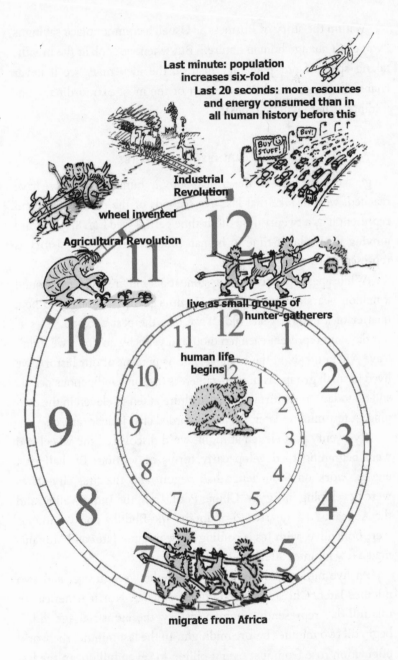

Figure 8.3. Here 240,000 years of human history are represented as a single day. Each hour represents 10,000 years, each minute 166 years.

The last third of a minute of this day of human history has seen an explosion not just of our population but also of our appetite for energy and resources. In the Business as Usual culture of industrialized economies, it is considered normal to consume thirty-two times the quantity of resources and to produce thirty-two times as much waste as those living in nonindustrial societies.[14] What is not being seen is how little fuel we have left and how much harm we are causing. Because our culture is not looking at where it is going, we are like the *Titanic*: moving very quickly but heading for a crash.

Learning to Reinhabit Time

A wonderful advantage of widening our time span is that doing so opens up a sense of possibility. If land-based mammals can return to the oceans and evolve into dolphins, then it is not such a stretch to think that modern human beings could return to a state of connectedness with the land and evolve into a wiser form of life.

The development of our species has been marked by, and driven by, discoveries that increase our capacity: speech, writing, tools, agriculture, the wheel, and now communication technologies that enable us to cooperate with people we've never even met living thousands of miles away. Could the discovery, or rediscovery, that ushers in the ecological age be the ability to reinhabit time?

Ecological intelligence involves thinking in terms of deep time — a temporal context that includes our whole story. We need to do this now because given our technologies, our actions have consequences extending millions, even billions, of years. Take the thousand tons of depleted uranium weaponry used in Iraq and Afghanistan. The cancer-causing aerosol it leaves behind has a half-life of four and a half billion years. That is as long as the age of Earth.

Learning to live in a larger timescape opens us to new allies and sources of strength. Our ancestors can be our allies, and we ourselves, as the ancestors of future generations, can play the role of ally to them as well. Perhaps these future generations have something to say to us.

Many of the advances we take for granted today were thought of as impossible before they were invented. Things we consider impossible today might still be developed in the future. Could future generations, for example, discover a way to communicate with us? And if so, what might they say? Perhaps they could only do this if we played our part too by extending ourselves forward in time to meet them. We can do this through our imagination. We don't know whether the communications we would receive this way are real or imagined — and we don't really need to know. They still offer useful guidance. Here is an exercise we often use in workshops, which we value for the richness it brings.

TRY THIS:
LETTER FROM THE SEVENTH GENERATION

The purpose of this exercise is to help us identify with future beings we might think of as the "seventh generation," that is, those living about two hundred years from now; to see our efforts from their perspective; and to receive counsel and courage.

Closing your eyes, imagine yourself journeying forward through time and identifying with a human being living two hundred years from now. You do not need to determine this person's circumstances, only to imagine that he or she is looking back at you from the time he or she inhabits. Imagine what this person would want to say to you. Open your mind and listen. Now begin putting words down on paper as if this future one were writing a letter just to you that starts: Dear [your name].

By giving future beings a voice, we bring them closer in a way that helps us be guided by their perspective. Hearing ourselves reply to them also helps us to step into a larger view of time. This next exercise invites us to reply to questions asked by future beings.

TRY THIS: LETTER TO THE FUTURE[15]

Write a reply to three questions you have received from future beings. Assume that important changes (i.e., the Great Turning) took place in the early twenty-first century that allowed human life to continue, and that those living in the future know about what happened in our time.

1. Ancestor, I hear stories about the period you are living in, with wars and preparations for war, with some people absurdly rich while huge numbers are starving and homeless, poisons in the seas and soil and air, the dying of many species. We're still experiencing the effects of all that. How much of this do you know about? And what is it like for you to live with this knowledge?

2. Ancestor, we have songs and stories that tell of what you and your friends did back then for the Great Turning. They don't tell us how you got started. You must have felt lonely and confused sometimes, especially at the beginning. What were the first steps you took?

3. Ancestor, I know you didn't stop with those first actions on behalf of life on Earth. Where did you find the strength to continue working so hard, despite all the obstacles and discouragements?

We can bring deep time to mind as we go about our daily lives. Even as we wash the dishes, pay the bills, go to meetings, and so on, we can school ourselves to be aware, now and then, of the hosts of ancestral and future beings surrounding us like a cloud of witnesses. We can remember the vaster story of our planet and let it imbue the most ordinary acts with meaning and purpose. Each of us is an intrinsic part of that story, like a cell in a larger organism. And in this story, each of us has a role to play. As we move into the Going Forth stage of the spiral, we begin to focus on that role.

PART THREE

Going Forth

CHAPTER NINE

Catching an Inspiring Vision

On August 28, 1963, Martin Luther King Jr. delivered one of the best-known speeches in history. Half a century later, the words *I have a dream* are still linked to the vision he shared that day.[1] King described a future in which black and white children would join hands as brothers and sisters and in which his own children would be judged by the "content of their character" rather than the color of their skin. He was identifying a destination that could be reached, a reality that could be created. In the 1960s the idea that an African American might one day become president of the United States would have been dismissed as "just dreaming." But just look at the impact that kind of dreaming can have.

Our dreams and visions for the future are essential for navigating through life because they give us a direction to move in. As the Roman philosopher Seneca once remarked, "If one does not know to which port one is sailing, no wind is favorable." Moreover, moving toward a destination that excites and inspires us energizes our journey, puts wind in our sails, and strengthens our determination to overcome obstacles. The ability to "catch" an inspiring vision is therefore key to staying motivated. When we're moved by a vision that we share with others, we become part of a community with a common purpose.

Inspiration is often thought of as a fleeting experience striking us in lucky moments or as a rare strength found in the small number of people thought of as "visionaries." In this chapter we look at how we can foster vision and inspiration using learnable skills. The insights and practices discussed here can help all of us become more inspired and visionary. They strengthen our capacity for going forth in the adventure of the Great Turning.

How Our Imagination Gets Switched Off

From an early age, we are schooled in a worldview that values facts over fantasies. The term *dreamer* is used as a dismissive put-down when someone's ideas are considered unrealistic; daydreaming in the classroom can even be a punishable offense. To develop our visioning ability, let's start by recognizing how it has become so undervalued. As Quaker futurist Elise Boulding comments: "Several generations of children have had daydreaming bred out of them. Our literacy is confined to numbers and words. There is no image literacy."[2]

With decades of research into how the brain works, we're beginning to understand that our two cerebral hemispheres function in different ways.[3] While the left side thinks in terms of words and rational logic, the right side works more with images and patterns, helping us to integrate complex information and to sense the larger shape of things. Since our educational system focuses almost exclusively on words and numbers, it is as though we are being taught to use only half our brain. A simple first step in developing our visioning ability is to recognize it as a form of intelligence that is both valuable and learnable.

To underline the crucial importance of visioning, consider how many aspects of our present reality started out as someone's dream. There was a time when much of America was a British colony, when women didn't have the vote, and when the slave trade was seen as essential to the economy. To change something, we need to first hold in our mind and heart the possibility that it could be different. Stephen Covey, in his best-selling book *The Seven Habits of Highly Effective People*, writes:

> "Begin with the end in mind" is based on the principle that
> all things are created twice. There's a mental or first creation,
> and physical or second creation to all things.[4]

Imagining possible futures is a surefire way to develop foresight. If we're only interested in "facts," we limit ourselves to looking at what has already happened, which is a bit like trying to drive a car by looking only in the rearview mirror. To avoid crashing, we need to look where we're going. Since we can't know for sure what will happen, we are limited to considering possibilities, based on applying a combination of experience, awareness of trends, and imagination. While experience equips us well for dealing with familiar situations, our imagination is essential in formulating creative responses to new challenges.

LIBERATING OUR IMAGINATION

A design principle that boosts creative thinking is "what comes before how." First identify *what* you'd like to happen; working out *how* comes later. If we exclude options just because we can't immediately see how they can happen, we block out many of the more exciting possibilities that might inspire us. An important distinction is to be made between the creative phase, in which we generate ideas and possibilities, and the editing phase, in which we choose and evaluate them. Placing an embargo on editing in this first stage liberates our creativity.

Our intention in the creative phase is to catch a vision so compelling that it touches us emotionally. To remain motivated during difficult times, we need to *really* want our vision to happen. When what we hope for seems beyond our power, however, we are likely to hear a voice inside us saying, "There's no point even thinking about this; it just isn't going to happen." To hold on to an inspiring vision, we need to stop ourselves from shooting it down inside our minds before it even has a chance to take form. What helps here is recognizing the difference between static and process thinking.

Static thinking assumes that reality is fixed and solid, resistant to change. When people say things such as "the problem is human nature, it is never going to change" or "you can't change the system," they're taking this approach. They are viewing situations as if they are like pictures hanging on a wall: if a new idea or way of doing things isn't already in the picture, it is seen as unrealistic (see Fig. 9.1). This view limits our sense of what is possible; if nothing inspiring is on the horizon, we can easily fall into apathy and resignation.

Figure 9.1. Static thinking sees reality as fixed and resistant to change.

With process thinking, we view reality more as a flow in which everything is continually moving from one state to another. Each moment, like a frame in a movie, is slightly different from the one before. These tiny changes from frame to frame generate the larger changes seen over time (see Fig. 9.2). If something is not in the picture at the moment, that doesn't mean it won't be later on. This way of conceiving reality sees existence as an evolving story rather than as predefined. Because we can never know for sure how the future will turn out, it makes more sense to focus on what we'd like to have happen, and then to do our bit to make it more likely. That's what Active Hope is all about.

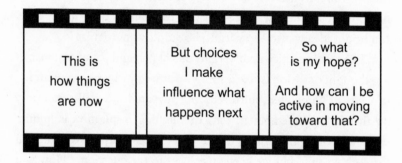

Figure 9.2. Process thinking: each moment is like a frame in a movie.

Practices That Help Us Catch Inspiration

There was once an inventor who sat for hours every day in a special soundproofed room. With a pencil in his hand and a pad of paper on his desk, he was waiting for ideas. When they came, he would make a note and then return to his waiting. This inventor is modeling three practices that can help us catch an inspiring vision.

The first is simply creating space. When we're too busy, our attention is so occupied that there is little room for anything new to enter. That is why people often remark that their most inspiring moments come when they are on vacation, out for a walk, or taking a shower. Allowing ourselves quiet moments, even to daydream, opens a space into which inspiring thoughts can flow. Such pauses can be surprisingly productive: Edison came up with many of his inventions while lying on a couch in his workshop. It was a daydream about a snake eating its tail that led German chemist Friedrich Kekulé to discover the ring structure of benzene molecules.

The second practice for catching inspiration brings together two tools freely available to us all: intention and attention. By placing himself in the soundproofed room, the inventor was making himself fully available to any creative impulses that might arise. His heightened alertness was like that of a cat waiting by a mouse hole. If a bright idea was to show itself, he didn't want to miss it.

The third practice involved his use of pen and paper. An inspiring thought or vision is like a seed — for it to grow into something, it needs to be planted, nurtured, and revisited often. We can only do that if we remember it. Part of catching inspiration is finding some way of holding on to it. We don't necessarily have to do that through writing, but we need an answer to the question, "How will I remember this a year from now?"

These three practices are the key ingredients of a guidance system that helps us find and follow the purposes that call us. There are many different ways of making space, of focusing our intention to catch an inspiring vision, and of anchoring what comes up so that we don't forget it. We'll be looking at a few approaches in more detail; it is worth experimenting with a range of them to find the ones that suit you best. The core principle here is that we don't have to just passively wait for inspiration; rather, we can play an active role in inviting it in. We can also train ourselves to become better at this, developing the habit and skill of tuning in to visionary signals.

Since the best way of anchoring a vision is to act on it and make it part of our lives, we need a way of linking our larger hopes with specific steps we can take. Visioning therefore involves three closely related levels:

1. *What?*

When looking at a specific situation, what would you like to see happen?

2. *How?*

How do you see this coming about? This stage involves describing the steps needed for the larger vision to occur and possible pathways by which these steps can take place.

3. *My Role?*

The first level identifies the desired destination, the second level maps out the story of getting there, and the third identifies your role in this story: What can you do to help the vision come about?

IMAGING THE FUTURE WE HOPE FOR

Feeling that the peace movement was clearer about what it was against than what it was for, Quaker futurist Elise Boulding developed a workshop called Imaging a World without Weapons. Its structured process moves through the three levels of visioning we've described. Here is how she describes it:

> There are two basic components to this type of imaging. The first is intentionality. We must allow ourselves not only to wish for but to intend the good. Our intentions about the future must be serious, so the first exercise in the imaging workshop is to make a list of things we want to see happen in the world thirty years into the future. We choose thirty years because it is far enough into the future so something can have happened, and near enough so that many of us will live into

that time. Participants must make their own lists. The items on it become their intentions.

The second component of imaging involves unlocking the total store of imagery in our mental warehouses.... To help participants get into that fantasying mode, the second exercise is to step into a childhood memory. Participants are asked to pick a happy one. I often go back to age nine and climb an apple tree in our yard. It is essential to use all one's inward senses in experiencing the scene; see the colors, feel the textures, smell the smells, hear the sounds, note the expressions on peoples' faces.... After a couple of minutes of remembering, each participant turns to a neighbor and describes where he or she has been, then listens to where the neighbor has been. Sharing the experience helps to clarify the memory.

It is this type of imaging you do when you image the world thirty years from now. You will see a world without weapons around you with the same vividness, as fragments from your stored experiences get recombined in a kind of movie reel inside your head.[5]

As preparation for moving into our preferred version of the future, the third stage of the workshop invites us to imagine ourselves standing in front of a huge, thick hedge stretching as far as we can see to the left and right. On the other side of this lies the world we hope for thirty years from now, where the intentions we identified in the first stage have been realized. We can move through or over the hedge any way we want and have a good look around. The goal is to be an observer and to collect information that can be reported back on.

After the imaging, we are invited to share with others what we have experienced. The more specific our observations are, the more real the image becomes to the person we're describing it to. So rather than using generalizations such as "no one is hungry," we are encouraged to be specific in describing what we see or hear. Each of us only sees a fragment of this potential future, so the next and fourth part of the workshop involves piecing together information yielded by different people's imaging to build a more coherent picture of what this future offers. How are decisions made? How does education work? The imaging provides clues that groups can build on. Boulding continues:

> We are in no way prophesying or predicting or compelling the future by this kind of imaging, any more than we are compelling the future when we pray. The enactment of the future depends on what we do, how we individually and collectively respond to what we envision.[6]

There are two more parts to the workshop. After spending time working together on developing a vision of our preferred future, we need to remember how we got there. Standing in the world thirty years from now, we look back at how the changes we have just envisioned were brought about. Moving back year by year, what happened? As we trace back to the present moment, we reconstruct a history of the preceding thirty years from the perspective of this possible future.

Finally, we need to see the role we play in this process. Looking at the different areas of our lives, what are we doing that helps build the future we hope for? There will be many things, and some might stand out — what are they?

IMAGINARY HINDSIGHT

A powerful mental shift takes place when we stop telling ourselves why something can't happen. When we can envision a hoped-for future, we strengthen our belief that it is possible. By inhabiting this vision with all our senses, imagining what colors and shapes we see, the expressions on people's faces, the sounds we hear, the smells, taste, and feel of this future, we bring ourselves there in a way that activates our creative, visionary, and intuitive faculties. As the poet Rumi once wrote: "Close both eyes to see with the other eye."[7]

Research has shown that when people approach a problem by imagining that it has already been solved and then look back from this imagined future, they are more creative and detailed in describing potential solutions.[8] Rob Hopkins used this "imaginary hindsight" approach when founding the Transition movement. He told us:

> The idea didn't emerge fully formed all at once. It was more a case of thinking "I wonder what would happen if..." and then imagining what a permaculture response to the challenge of peak oil would look like, particularly a response that could easily catch on around the world.

The idea that each community could develop its own "energy descent plan" grew out of this visioning process. The starting point is an image of what a community would look like if it were no longer dependent on oil. How would it function? What would people eat? How would its economy, healthcare, and education systems work? Then a trail is traced back in time from that possible future, marking key developments along the way. The pathway sketched out offers the beginnings of an energy descent plan by which the community can wean itself off oil dependence. Finally, as in Boulding's model, we end in the present, with our lives here and now, looking forward and identifying how we can play our part in the transition process.

Imaginary hindsight can be applied to a range of timescales. If we're facing a challenge in the next twenty-four hours, we can imagine its successful resolution a day from now, and then look back from that point at what we did. The story of how we rose to the challenge directs our attention to the steps we need to take.

THE STORYTELLERS CONVENTION

It can be fun as well as illuminating to play with this imaginary hindsight process through the use of storytelling. When giving talks, Chris sometimes guides audiences in imaginary time travel to a hoped-for future hundreds of years from now. He invites them into the fantasy that they are at a gathering of storyteller-historians where, in pairs, they take turns sharing their stories of the Great Turning. Taking just a few minutes each way, they tell the tales they may have heard as children, about that historic period in the early twenty-first century when human society seemed on the path to collective suicide. Though things didn't look too promising at first, a widespread awakening occurred, and huge numbers of people rose to the challenge of creating the life-sustaining society familiar to the storytellers now. After sharing their stories, the audience travels back to the present time, carrying with them a deepened sense of the mythic adventure we are part of. While the stories told are fantasies, some may be close to realities that will occur. When we carry our desired future inside us, it guides and acts through us, helping us bring it into being.

NIGHTMARES CAN INSPIRE US TOO

We have been using the word *dream* to refer to the futures we hope for. However, it is not only positive visions that guide us. Our nightmares can alert us to dangerous conditions and summon us to respond on behalf of life. In the early years of the Work That Reconnects, Joanna had a particularly lucid and disturbing dream. Engaged at the time in a citizen's lawsuit to stop faulty storage of high-level waste, she had been reviewing public health statistics in localities around nuclear power plants. One night, before going to bed, she had leafed through baby pictures of her three children to find a snapshot for her daughter's high school yearbook. That night she had a nightmare:

I behold the three of them as they appeared in the old photos. My husband and I are journeying with them across an unfamiliar landscape. The terrain becomes dreary, treeless, and strewn with rocks. Little Peggy can barely clamber over the boulders in the path. Just as the going is getting very difficult, even frightening, I suddenly realize that by some thoughtless but unalterable prearrangement, their father and I must leave them. I can see the grimness of the way that lies ahead of them, bleak as a Martian landscape and with a flesh-burning sickness in the air. I am maddened with sorrow that my children must face this ordeal without me. I kiss them each and tell them we will meet again, but I know no place to name where we will meet. Perhaps another planet, I say. Innocent of terror, they try to reassure me, ready to be off. Removed and from a height in the sky, I watch them go — three small solitary figures trudging across that angry wasteland, holding one another by the hand and not stopping to look back. In spite of the widening distance, I see with a surrealist's precision the ulcerating of their flesh. I see how the skin bubbles and curls back to expose raw tissue, as they doggedly go forward, the boys helping their little sister across the rocks.

When Joanna mentioned this dream in an article, the dread of a mother seeing her children left behind in a barren, toxic world struck a strong chord with readers, many of them writing to share similar nightmares and their own fears for our world.

THE DREAM OF THE EARTH

When we think of ourselves as interconnected parts of a larger web of life, just as we may feel the Earth crying within us, perhaps we can experience the Earth dreaming within us too. Within the framework of systems thinking and the ecological self, this makes perfect sense. If self is thought of as a stream of consciousness with many currents, then inspired dreams and visionary moments are simply times of increased connectedness with the deeper flows of our collective identity.

The idea that our dreams, those we have when awake and asleep, can tap into deeper sources of wisdom is found in many cultures. In the Bible, the Pharaoh's dream of seven lean cows eating seven fat cows was interpreted by Joseph as a warning that seven years of famine would follow an equal period of abundance. In the indigenous culture of North America, the term *medicine dream* is used to describe the guiding visions that come in our dreams. In *The Dream of the Earth*, Thomas Berry writes, "Such dream experiences are so universal and so important in the psychic life of the individual and of the community that techniques of dreaming are taught in some societies."[9]

The simplest technique is just to pay attention to our dreams, to see them as significant. We might make a note of them while they are still fresh in our mind. Some cultures have early-morning gatherings to share their dreams of the night before and draw out possible meanings. Our dreams can tell us things, but only if we listen to them.

If we're able to receive guiding signals from our larger ecological self, then rather than catching inspired visions, perhaps we could say it is the inspiring vision that catches us. In every situation latent possibilities are waiting to come into being. In dreamy visionary states we get glimpses of these possibilities; when these visionary images land in us, they can work through us and take form in our actions. The same vision can catch several people and bring them together in a community of shared purpose. In this view, a visionary impulse is not something we invent; it is something we serve.

While this concept of guiding visionary signals fits comfortably in both spiritual and systems perspectives, it clashes with the ultra-individualistic worldview of the industrialized world. In this model, thinking and intelligence are located within individuals; if someone comes up with a good idea, that idea is regarded as their property. When the ownership of ideas is privatized, innovations that could help our world are often kept secret until they can be exploited for personal or corporate benefit. What would happen to a brain if separate groups of neurons took this approach?

Thinking happens through brain cells rather than within them, and intelligence is an emergent property of cells working together as a larger whole. Viewing ourselves as similar to brain cells opens us up an entirely new way of thinking about intelligence. Co-intelligence, which we touched on in chapter 6, is defined by the Co-Intelligence Institute as "accessing the wisdom of the whole on behalf of the whole."[10] If we think of ourselves as part of the team of life on Earth, could we access the wisdom of our world for the benefit of all?

Co-intelligence arises when we share ideas and visions we find inspiring, making room to hear what moves other people too. This is how visions catch on and spread through a culture with amazing speed.

TRY THIS: SHARING INSPIRATION

The following open sentence can be used as a round in groups, as a prompt to conversation with a small group of friends, as a starting point for personal journaling, or as something to include in letters to friends: "Something that inspires me at the moment is..."

CO-INTELLIGENCE IN PROGRESSIVE BRAINSTORMING

A progressive brainstorm process that Joanna has used in workshops provides a good example of co-intelligence arising. This process is a great way of harnessing group creativity in moving from a larger, general goal to specific steps that participants can take. It can be fun and energizing to recruit a few interested friends to try this process together. The first stage is to identify a goal to work toward. Each person daydreams for a few minutes about what he or she would like to see in a life-sustaining society. These features are then listed on a big sheet of paper (see Box 9.1).

Box 9.1. Stage 1: Our Vision for a Life-Sustaining Society

- clean air
- renewable energy
- constructive processes to deal with conflict
- lifestyles of voluntary simplicity
- widespread ecological awareness

For the next stage, the group selects one of these and has a brainstorm process generating responses to the question "What would be needed for this?" As the goal of brainstorming is to spark creative thinking, it is guided by three rules: first, we don't censor, explain, or justify our ideas; second, we don't evaluate or criticize the ideas of others; and third, we save discussion for later. We're creating options, not editing them (see Box 9.2, which takes "clean air" as an example).

Once a list has been generated, one of the options is chosen, and the process is repeated, with a brainstorm exploring the question, "What would be needed for this to happen?" Each time this is repeated, the steps identified become closer to us and easier to take.

Box 9.2. Stage 2: What Would Be Needed for Clean Air?

- fewer cars and trucks
- no incinerators
- scrubbers on smokestacks
- more renewable energy investment
- more concern about health impacts of air pollution

The goal is to end up with a list of practical steps that anyone in the room can take (see Box 9.3, which takes "fewer cars and trucks" as an example). When this process is in full swing, you can feel the group thinking and strategizing through each of its members.

Box 9.3. Stage 3: What Would Be Needed
for Fewer Cars and Trucks?

- pedestrian malls
- bicycle lanes
- higher fuel prices
- more public transportation
- greater use of carpooling

CHOOSING AND BEING CHOSEN

With every theme we take up, there will be a range of possible pathways for actions in which we could play a role. With so many options, how do we choose where to invest our energy? The challenge is to listen for the vision that calls us most strongly and to recognize that to follow this well, we will need to refine our focus so as not to dissipate our energy. Like seedlings that need thinning out, we need to choose which visions we support, and then clear space around them so that they have room to develop and thrive.

There may be a few special times in our lifetime when we experience such a strong intuitive pull toward a course of action that we know it to be the right thing for us to do. Even when the odds seem against us, we feel these powerful summonings deep in our hearts and we are drawn to respond.

In the model of co-intelligence, we're never alone in these endeavors. A larger story is taking place, and we've just chosen, or been chosen, to play a particular role in it. If we trust in a larger intelligence, we can open to the support of many allies and helpers who will play their roles too. Joseph Campbell wrote, "Follow your bliss...and doors will open where there were no doors before."[11]

We don't make these visions happen — we just play our part in them. To do that, we need to keep our vision, and our commitment to it, strong inside us; then we can follow wherever it takes us. Here's an example from Joanna's life.

JOURNEY TO TIBET

The vision took hold when a message arrived from a dear friend and teacher she had known for more than twenty years. A Tibetan lama in exile from the Chinese occupation of his homeland, Dugu Choegyal Rinpoche was based in northwest India with his refugee community of monks and laypeople. His friendship with Joanna began in the 1960s when he was eighteen and Joanna, twice his age, was living in India with her family as part of the American Peace Corps. Over the years, through Choegyal's stories and luminous paintings, the Tibet he had left behind became very real to Joanna. He never expected to see it again, but in 1981 and for the next half-dozen years a softening in Chinese occupation policy allowed lamas in exile to visit the homeland. Choegyal Rinpoche's trip to his homeland in Kham in eastern Tibet was so rewarding to him and so useful to his people that he proceeded to plan another visit in 1987; this time he asked Joanna, now living in California, to join him there.

I wrote back an immediate YES! and said that my husband Fran and daughter Peggy would be coming too. Choegyal's paintings of his homeland were so vivid to me that I could picture being right there in the high green hills of Kham, and just as compelling were the plans we had been talking about. Choegyal was eager to restore his monastic center from the ruins left by the Cultural Revolution, gathering some of the monks who had gone into hiding; and for the laypeople he would build a Tibetan-language school and a craft center for traditional arts. Having been inspired by my stories of the village self-help movement in Sri Lanka, he called his vision, which had now become mine as well, the Eastern Tibet Self-Help Project.

I was fifty-eight years old then, and our daughter would turn twenty-six on the trip. The only Tibetan map I found that featured the region of Kham unfolded awkwardly to a good three feet wide. On it, Kham, about the size of Switzerland, was no bigger than my palm. It showed the route we planned to take, approaching Tibet from the east through Szechuan. Taking over the dining room, Peggy and I assembled oxygen tablets, water filters, rolls of film, vitamins, Band-Aids, belly medicines, trail mix, high-altitude lip gels, sunglasses, and gifts for our Tibetan hosts. We each bought lightweight mountain boots — in beige and navy for Peg and Fran, aqua for me.

We secured our Chinese visas but not the papers allowing us to enter the Autonomous Region of Tibet, which until recently had been closed off. The consular agent in San Francisco assured us that we could obtain these Alien Travel Permits after we landed in Beijing. We banked on this hope as the three of us checked our bulging backpacks and sleeping bags and settled into our seats on the Air China plane.

At each successive stop — Beijing, Chengdu, and the smaller towns farther west where we pressed on for days by bus and hired car — we beseeched every Chinese authority we could find for the permits to travel in Tibet. They all refused. Our last hope was Der'ge, the town closest to the Yangtze River, which was the border itself. But there the police not only refused us the permits, they also ordered us to leave the entire area within two days.

The determination to join Choegyal in his homeland was as strong as ever. It was even intensified by the efforts we had already expended, and by the tantalizing proximity to Kham in the Autonomous Region of Tibet, barely fifty miles away on the other side of the Yangtze. So on hearing that a high lama I knew, long based in the West, was passing through Der'ge on his way out of Tibet, I sought his help. Akong Rinpoche had no hope to offer, though he had good relations with Chinese authorities. Indeed, two border officials, coming from their duties at the Yangtze checkpoint, dropped by for tea while we were there. When Akong Rinpoche sounded them out on our behalf, their answer was curt and final.

Someone else, however, was in the room, quietly listening. Tenzin was a young Tibetan from Der'ge, about to return to his studies in Berlin. He overheard me say at one point, "I will do anything to get in. Anything." Tenzin repeated those words back to me when he tracked us down that night. "If that is so, you must love your lama very much. I have a plan for you, if you are willing to try it." The plan involved a local man he knew and trusted, a man who had a tractor. We met this man within the hour, when Tenzin brought him to meet us and look at our map. Since we spoke no Tibetan, we used gestures only, and his were few. It was best not to know his real name, so Fran, Peggy, and I, among ourselves, called him Tractor.

The next morning when we met him in the marketplace he barely glanced at us; impassively, he nodded toward the narrow wagon hitched to his three-wheeled tractor. Eight others, including a couple of monks, had climbed aboard and now pulled us up to sit beside them on the narrow side planks. Soon we were slowly rumbling westward out of Der'ge along fields of barley stubble shining golden under a spanking-blue sky. Our wagon mates' smiles and chatter made it seem as if we were all heading off on a picnic.

When we stopped on a high shoulder above the Yangtze three hours later, all but one of our traveling companions had left us, replaced by heavy bags of barley pulled aboard at recent stops. Peering downriver we saw the far end of the bridge, sentry boxes, figures moving. Pulling us quickly out of view, Tractor gestured us onto the wagon's narrow floor and hushed us into silence. No sooner did we lie down — we could only manage it on our sides, spoon-fashion, Fran curled around my back, me around Peggy's — than the sacks of barley landed on top of us, pinning us down in airless darkness.

With Tractor's companion sitting on top of us, the weight was crushing, but the struggle to breathe was the hardest thing. As we jolted down the road headfirst, my chest heaved and hammered for air. I prayed to my lungs: be still. I prayed to pass out before exploding in panic. I prayed that Peggy not suffocate. After a turn and a couple of stops, shrill Chinese voices were shouting just a foot or two away. The wagon started up again, made another turn, finally stopping. Sheer gratitude eased the breathing even before the sacks were pulled off, but then we saw Tractor's alarm. In pantomime he conveyed what had happened: the rifles aimed at his head, the sacks at the end of the wagon pulled aside, and beneath them three pairs of American boots — those beige and navy and aqua boots.

The wonder was that we hadn't been hauled out on the spot and tossed into jail. For that, we figured, we could probably thank those border officials who took tea with Akong Rinpoche and knew that three American friends of his were attempting to cross the border. Another wonder was that Tractor did not abandon us forthwith to save himself from dangerous trouble. Instead he doggedly persisted in trying to get us across the Yangtze. By late afternoon he had brought us nine miles downriver from the bridge, turning off the road onto a steep dirt track toward the water's edge. Switching off the motor, he walked us with our gear to a grove of trees where a rowboat lay hidden. As daylight dimmed, he ferried us across.

The skiff was shallow, the current strong. It took two scary trips to get our bodies and packs to the farther shore, all the while in full view of Szechuan's one paved road along the Yangtze. On the rocks below the steep, wooded bank, we turned to say good-bye to Tractor. He was coatless now and shivering. He knew, as we did, that we had to move fast if we were to find our way north to where the road came off the bridge and then head farther into Kham before dawn. He pointed to the river, the sky. Yes, we understood, keep the river on our right, follow the stars. I touched his arm, trying uselessly to thank him, trying to memorize the face of this man, whose name I didn't know. I wanted to be able to recognize that face someday, on a street, in a crowd.

Four weeks later Fran, Peg, and I are seated once more aboard an Air China plane, this time on our way home. In my lap lie notebooks filled with jottings, figures, lists, sketches. Rough estimates of cement and wood to be procured are mixed in with drawings by Choegyal Rinpoche of the school he envisages, and dimensions of the looms he proposes for the craft center. Names of the families who'll volunteer labor figure alongside those who have agreed to contribute rocks for the walls, or food for the building crews. I know all this will serve me well in writing the grant proposals for the modest funds we need. And I know that the Eastern Tibet Self-Help Project has already begun.

Equally precious to me are the faces that drift before me, as the plane's lights dim for the night. In my mind's eye I see Tractor and Tenzin and the others who helped us in essential ways we could not have foreseen. I see the Khampa horseman whose campfire we found soon after our river crossing. With his teenage son and two horses, he brought us through the moonless night on cliff-edge trails above the Yangtze. I see the tiny old woman from the village we reached by sunrise. No one there would notice or speak to us, the Chinese seeming to be more repressive near the border. But after we had walked on out of sight, and waited long vain hours for a lift, she appeared, hobbling slowly down the road. In a brass kettle as heavy as she was, she was bringing us tea — the first warm food in two days. I see the truck driver who took the risk to break the rules and take on three foreigners who'd been marooned for days in the mud and grease of a transport yard. And, of course, I see my old friend Choegyal Rinpoche, greeting us with calm pleasure, as if he hadn't doubted for a minute that we would make our way to him.

CHAPTER TEN

Daring to Believe It Is Possible

In 1785 Thomas Clarkson, a student at Cambridge University, entered an essay competition; the topic was slavery. As he researched the subject, he was horrified by what he discovered about the transatlantic slave trade. His essay won first prize, but its content so disturbed him he found it difficult to sleep. In his diary he wrote: "In the daytime I was uneasy. In the night I had little rest. I sometimes never closed my eye-lids for grief."[1]

Abandoning his plans to become an Anglican minister, he decided instead to join a small group of Quakers campaigning on the issue. Two years later, Clarkson was one of the dozen people whose meeting in a London print shop kicked off the Society for Effecting the Abolition of the Slave Trade.

Along with William Wilberforce and a few other committed campaigners, Clarkson had caught an inspiring vision. At the time, the odds seemed completely stacked against them. Slavery was accepted as a normal part of life. The slave trade was well established, and there were powerful vested interests opposing any change. In the British House of Commons, the idea of abolishing the slave trade was described as "unnecessary, visionary and impracticable"; repeated attempts by Wilberforce to bring in a new law were blocked. Such was the opposition that Clarkson was nearly killed when he was attacked by a mob on the docks of Liverpool.

When following the path of an inspiring vision, we are likely to encounter the voice dismissing what we hope for as unnecessary or impractical. The greater the gap between present reality and what we would like to have happen, the louder this voice will be. Yet stories like those of Clarkson and Wilberforce remind us that when we dare to believe our vision is possible, and dare also to act on this belief, extraordinary changes can take place. In 1807 the British Parliament passed a law making the slave trade illegal within the British Empire. As other countries followed, slavery became outlawed almost everywhere within little more than a lifetime. As Nelson Mandela once said of changes like this: "It always seems impossible until it is done."

This chapter explores how to protect ourselves from disillusionment if we are struggling to believe that what we hope for is possible. We'll look at what helps us move from just thinking about a vision to taking steps to bring it about, and also at what strengthens our resolve to do this even when the odds seem stacked against us.

FACING THE CHALLENGE OF DISBELIEF

When we have a vision that inspires us and we feel ourselves moving toward it, the combination of purpose and progress is energizing. Unfortunately, the experience many of us have when acting to preserve our world isn't always like this. The facts of climate change, habitat loss, mass extinction of species, and mass starvation of people are hugely discouraging. When we're working for causes that seem to be getting nowhere, that suffer setbacks and reversals, that face well-funded obstruction and deeply entrenched resistance, it is hard to sustain the belief that what we hope for is possible. Yet without this, without the spark of conviction that our actions can really make a difference, it is difficult to keep going.

We need to name this challenge, because the risk with recurring frustration, failure, and disappointment is that they will wear down our resolve. It is painful to keep hold of a vision if we don't believe we can make meaningful progress toward it. The reference points that support our sense of possibility are therefore crucial. Let's look at five of these:

- inspiring examples from history
- the phenomenon of discontinuous change
- facing your threshold guardians
- our own experiences of perseverance
- witnessing the Great Turning happening through us

Inspiring Examples from History

It took Clarkson and Wilberforce more than twenty years of campaigning before they saw a law against the slave trade passed.[2] They were challenging the Business as Usual mode of their day, and while they had periods of hard-earned popular support, there were also times when their cause looked completely hopeless. In the early 1790s, the French Revolution and subsequent war with France led to a clampdown on political opposition in Britain. Harsh new laws forbade gatherings of more than fifty people unless they had permission from a local magistrate. If a magistrate declared a meeting illegal, and more than twelve people were still gathered an hour later, they could be sentenced to death. The abolition committee gave up its London office and went for seven years without meeting. Clarkson had a nervous breakdown, and the campaign went into decline.

There is a saying that important changes often go through three phases. First they are regarded as a joke. Then they are treated as a threat. Finally, they become accepted as normal. Historical examples of changes moving through this sequence provide an important reference point for us. If it is a struggle for you to believe that what you hope for is possible, know that others have felt this way too. Thanks to the people who kept alive the spark of their convictions through periods of ridicule and persecution, changes that were laughed at, actively suppressed, or dismissed as hopeless dreams have now become accepted as normal parts of our reality. Here are some examples.

Box 10.1. Aspects of Current Reality
Once Dismissed as Hopeless Dreams

- Women have the vote in nearly every country in the world.
- An African American can become US president.
- Apartheid came to an end in South Africa.
- Most people now accept that the earth orbits around the sun.

Lucy Stone organized the first National Women's Rights Convention in Worcester, Massachusetts, in 1850. She never lived to see women finally get the vote in the United States in 1920, but that didn't stop her from working her whole life to make that happen. Nelson Mandela was imprisoned for more than twenty-five years before eventually becoming South Africa's first black president in 1994. Galileo was branded a heretic for believing Earth revolved around the sun, had his writings banned, and spent the last eight years of his life under house arrest. When we experience frustration, failure, or obstruction, we need to remember that we are part of a very fine historical tradition.

Could it be that one day future generations will look back and wonder how we dared to believe we could create a life-sustaining society, and dared also to bring it about? For that to happen, we need the capacity to tolerate frustration. Rather than seeing frustration and failure as evidence that we're pursuing a hopeless cause, we can reframe them as natural, even necessary, features in the journey of social change.

Why might failure and frustration be necessary parts of the journey? Because if we stick only with what we know how to do, what we're comfortable with and confident about, we limit ourselves to the old, familiar ways rather than developing new capacities. When we learn a new skill, we tend at first to get it wrong, gaining experience through our mishaps. Learning is a process that begins with not knowing. The good news about frustration and failure is they show that we have dared to step outside our comfort zones and to rise to a challenge that stretches us. What we're doing here is reframing frustration and failure in a way that encourages us to persist rather than to give up. By persisting we are more likely to experience the positive surprise of the next reference point.

The Phenomenon of Discontinuous Change

With issues such as climate change and peak oil, we don't have seventy years, or even twenty years, to bring about the changes needed. Our problems are urgent and demand much more rapid action. Given our current slow pace of progress, it can be hard to see how we will do it.

If we look at change as something that happens incrementally at a steady, predictable rate, in which the progress — or lack thereof — in one decade gives a measure of what is likely to take place in the next, we can get very discouraged. But along with continuous change, there is also *discontinuous* change. Sudden shifts can happen in ways that surprise us; structures that appear as fixed and solid as the Berlin Wall can collapse or be dismantled in a very short time. An understanding of discontinuous change opens up a genuine sense of possibility.

Consider what happens to a bottle of water when it is left in the freezer. As it cools down, there is a steady, continuous change in its temperature. The water won't change much in appearance until it begins to get near the critical threshold of its freezing point. Then, as it passes this, an extraordinary process happens. Tiny crystals form, and when they do, other crystals form around those crystals, until there is a mass movement of crystallization in the water that rapidly changes state from liquid to solid. This is discontinuous change.

With discontinuous change, a threshold is crossed where rather than just more of the same happening, something different occurs. There's a jump to a new level, an opening to a new set of possibilities. We might think it impossible that a small amount of water could crack something as hard as glass, but as the ice expands, it breaks the bottle.

Even when we don't see a visible result from our actions, we may be adding to an unseen change that moves the situation closer to a threshold where something crystallizes. When a line is crossed and something new starts to happen, the change may appear to come out of nowhere.

Discontinuous changes can be triggered by quite small events. When you're close to a threshold, one tiny step can take you over it. An example of this is when a tipping point is reached and a critical mass of people starts to believe a change can happen. If those who are undecided have been hovering on the edge beforehand, waiting to see what happens, something small can tip the balance and nudge them into giving their support. Before this threshold is crossed, the change may seem unlikely. Yet only a short while later, everyone wants to join in.

Each time we take a step forward, we don't know how this action will interact with the actions of others to create an entirely new set of circumstances. When one change makes other changes more likely, a cascade of events can be triggered that leads to a breakthrough. Like a snowball rolling down hill, each movement forward adds momentum. With synergy, unforeseeable properties arise as if by magic.

Discontinuous shifts can happen in both directions. Just as new ways of thinking can catch people's imagination and pivotal innovations can unexpectedly take off, so too can tipping points bring about rapidly worsening conditions. While we face the very real danger of catastrophic collapse, we can also be poised on the edge of a major evolutionary leap.

We can't know how things will unfold. What we can do is make a choice about what we'd like to have happen, and then put ourselves fully behind that possibility. An inspiring wave of change is spreading through our world. The Great Turning is happening in our time, and we may already be participating in many ways. If we want this change to catch on more thoroughly, deeply, and rapidly, how can we let it do so in our own lives? What thresholds do we need to cross? When we step over the line from one state to another, we take part in this shift.

Facing Your Threshold Guardians

When we catch our inspiring vision, we experience a call to adventure that pulls us into its service. There may be a treasured piece of forest we want to protect, a community project we want to support, or a valuable quality we wish to bring out in ourselves and others. But we will just about always bump into some kind of resistance or opposition. Mythologist Joseph Campbell coined the term *threshold guardian* to describe whatever is guarding or blocking the way.[3] Studying myths, legends, and adventure tales from all over the world, he mapped out a common plot structure that revolved around the tension between the impetus to follow the call to adventure and the threshold guardians in the way.

In fantasy adventures such as *The Lord of the Rings*, whenever there is a clear path to follow, there is always some kind of monster or other enemy about to appear on it. The hero or heroine then rises to the challenge by confronting, tricking, befriending, or bypassing the blocking entity in a way that allows the journey to continue. We can view our own lives similarly. When we're following our calls to adventure, thinking of obstacles as threshold guardians can draw out our creative response. Sarah, an activist with the Transition movement, described the impact doing this had on her:

> *I wanted to set up a Transition project in the city where I live. But I thought, "No way, it is too huge a project, I can't do that." Hearing the idea that our lives are like adventure stories changed the whole way I thought about this. It was a huge thing to do, and I wasn't sure it was possible, but that's the way these stories begin.*

Whenever Sarah was struggling, she'd say to herself, "This is my adventure; these are my threshold guardians." Rather than feeling defeated, she knew she needed to seek out allies, learn new skills, and not be put off when things weren't working out.

Adventure tales have been told for thousands of years, not just for their entertainment value but also because they pass on teachings that help us rise to challenges. Almost always, the protagonists find their way through by drawing on the fellowship of allies, by serving a purpose much bigger than themselves, by discovering strengths previously hidden from view, and by having enough humility to learn from others. Usually some mysterious force lends a hand. It could be a spiritual presence, the moral force of a value like justice, or, as in the film *Avatar*, the emergent power of an interconnected web of life.

Sometimes the threshold guardians have a tangible physical presence outside of us; for Joanna, following her powerful summoning to meet Choegyal Rinpoche in Tibet, the blocking force came in the form of the visa-refusing authorities and the Chinese border guards. But the thresholds we cross lie as much inside us as they do outside. For Sarah to step into her commitment to set up a Transition City initiative, she needed to find a way past the voice that said, "No way, it's too huge, I can't do that." This is the threshold guardian of disbelief.

It can help to imagine these blocking voices as characters standing in our way. Chris recently worked with some puppeteers to give visible expression to the common blocks of fear, cynicism, and disbelief. Fear took the form of an overprotective parent constantly warning of the dangers of stepping into anything new. The voice of cynicism was a dismissive distant relative who tore apart the value of any project considered. Finally, disbelief was personified by Professor Noway, the very clever character who has studied everything and knows precisely why there is no way we can succeed.

These characters sometimes have useful things to say. Listening to our fear can stop us from being too reckless, and a healthy skepticism protects us from getting involved in causes that don't ring true. Professor Noway might, from time to time, be right. When encountering the inner voice that would stop us, how do we know whether it is protecting us or blocking us? By listening to our own objections, and then scrutinizing and challenging them, we can counter our own resistance. When we undo the blocks that hold us back, we liberate our power to act. The next reference point illustrates this.

Our Own Experiences of Perseverance

Many of us will have struggled to make a change that seemed so difficult we wondered whether it was even possible. The times when we have eventually found a way through offer another important reference point of possibility. They remind us that when we hear the voice saying, "No way, I can't see it happening," we can sometimes prove Professor Noway wrong. Here Chris recounts an example of this from his own life.

In the late 1980s, I worked as an intern/junior hospital doctor in London. As was common practice then, my contract was for an average of eighty-eight hours a week, though some weeks I would work well over a hundred hours. Starting work at eight in the morning, I might not stop work till three in the morning the next day. But as I was still on call, I could be called back to work half an hour later, eventually getting to bed at five in the morning for a brief snatch of sleep that might only last an hour, before I was called back to the ward again. I would then continue throughout the day till my work finished at five that afternoon. I would work around the clock like this for two thirty-three-hour shifts most weeks, plus working during the day on the other weekdays. On top of this, every third weekend I would have a continuous stretch of duty of between fifty and eighty hours at a time. During some of these weekend shifts (which could extend from Friday morning till Monday afternoon), the longest period of uninterrupted sleep I had at any one time was ninety minutes.

When I started working like this, I found the conditions difficult to believe. I was surprised there wasn't a mass campaign to improve conditions, but nearly all the doctors I spoke to felt resigned and powerless. "We don't have the power here," I was told. "There is nothing we can do." As I asked around, nearly everyone agreed that although it was a crazy way to work, there was no point in trying to change things. First, any campaign would be doomed to fail because the system was so deeply entrenched; second, if you spoke out, you'd be threatening your career, because doctors were dependent on good references from their employers in order to get their next job. If you wanted to move forward in medicine, you had to put up with the hours and keep your mouth shut.

A small group of doctors weren't put off by these pressures and had set up a campaign. I immediately joined them. Together, we wrote letters to newspapers, organized lobbies of Parliament, and arranged meetings in hospitals. As the campaign began to grow, a television news team approached me for an interview. The evening before it was due to take place, I was phoned at home by a hospital manager. "If you go ahead with this," I was told, "you'll need to watch out for your future." The message was clear: speaking out was career suicide. Yet this was the fear that kept the system in place. If there was ever to be a change, it would require that people stick their necks out. So I went ahead.

Moving across that threshold of fear was liberating, and as other doctors started to speak out too, a small committed group set up a media campaign. When we carried out an overnight protest outside a London hospital, the issue became a major news story. Over the next year, there were more high-profile actions and lots of press coverage. Unfortunately, there was no change in our working conditions, and morale in the campaign group began to dip.

Suffering from severe sleep deprivation, I became clinically depressed. A friend who'd been a lawyer before studying medicine suggested legal action. Together we consulted a well-known barrister: in his opinion, there was no basis in law for a claim and attempting legal action could damage the campaign, since it might get laughed out of court. A second lawyer came to a similar verdict: "There's no precedent," he said.

Another friend, who was a lawyer, took a different view. She offered to help, free of charge, in attempting to secure an injunction to stop the hospital requiring me to work more than seventy-two hours in a week, or more than twenty-four consecutive hours without a protected period for sleep. Every employer had a legal obligation to provide a safe system of work; the health authority was failing in this because exhausted doctors were more likely to make mistakes, and sleep deprivation was a risk factor for depression. To maximize media coverage, the writ was served on a bank holiday, on Monday, just after I had finished my fifty-hour weekend shift.

Thirty journalists and six television crews were waiting outside the hospital. "Yawn this way," they called, as they took photos. The story made international headlines, and friends on the other side of the world saw the news on their televisions. As a media stunt, it worked brilliantly. But drawing attention to the issue wasn't enough to bring about the change that was needed.

At a court hearing, the claim was judged to be a frivolous action with no basis in law and was struck out. That could have been the end of it. But a leading barrister had stepped forward to offer his services for free. He believed there were grounds for an appeal, though if it were lost, I would be charged for the health authority's legal costs and I didn't have the funds to cover them. A newspaper article described our dilemma, and people starting sending in money. More than two hundred letters of support came flooding in, along with thousands of pounds in donations.

The doctors' union, the British Medical Association, was approached to see if they'd back the case, but their legal adviser said it didn't have a chance. In a newspaper interview, Lord Denning, the country's top judge, gave the same opinion. It would be unheard of, he said, for a court to declare that working too hard was illegal. Yet when I read the letters of support, including some from doctors who, like me, had felt so desperate they'd considered suicide, I knew I had to continue.

Taking a holiday in Scotland, one afternoon I momentarily fell asleep while driving. When I opened my eyes, I was on the wrong side of the road with a car speeding toward me. I swerved out of the way and my car went out of control, veered off the road, and crashed into a rock face. The car was totaled. Fortunately I escaped with just a graze to my knee. But the message seemed clear: if I continued working like this, driving myself on and on without adequate sleep, I was going to crash. Just a few days previously, I'd finished a working week of 112 hours.

The crash served as a wake-up call. The working conditions weren't just unpleasant; they had become a matter of life and death. Around that time, several young doctors had been killed in car accidents and sleep deprivation was suspected as a cause. I gave notice of my resignation and became more determined than ever to pursue the case. A few months later, the appeal succeeded. The ruling here was an important victory: it set a legal precedent establishing that it was unlawful for an employer to demand so much overtime as to bring foreseeable harm to health. At this point, the British Medical Association decided to back the case, and preparations for the trial began.

Over the next few years, the Health Authority made several more attempts to block the case on legal grounds. They even tried to take it to the House of Lords. But eventually a trial date was set for May 1995. It was to be a category A trial, meaning it was judged to be of great public significance. Just weeks before the trial was due to begin, the Health Authority offered an out-of-court settlement. They were concerned they might lose and wanted to avoid the costs of an expensive trial. They paid me a small damages award, plus all the legal costs. Along with the precedent set by the Court of Appeal ruling, this

settlement sent a powerful message to employers: they would
be financially vulnerable to negligence claims if they failed to
consider the health impact of excessive hours of work. The age
of hundred-hour workweeks was coming to an end. The case
was won.

When a change wants to happen, it looks for people to act
through. How do we know when a change wants to happen? We
feel the want inside us. There is a desire, a tugging at us to be involved. But that doesn't make the change inevitable, because standing in our way are all those who say we're wasting our time, that it
isn't possible, that it will be too hazardous. For the change to happen through us, we need to counter those voices. A shift can happen
within us when we break through a resistance that has been holding
us back.

Witnessing the Great Turning Happening through Us

When we see with new eyes, we recognize how every action has
significance, how the bigger story of the Great Turning is made up
of countless smaller stories of communities, campaigns, and personal actions. We don't know whether these changes will happen
fast enough to avoid collapse, but given the unpredictable nature
of discontinuous change, they just might. This is not the same as
being confident, but it does involve being open to the possibility of
success.

If you were freed from fear and doubt, what would you choose
to do for the Great Turning? Here is an action planning process
we use in our workshops. It will help you to identify some practical steps you can commit to taking in the next seven days. Seeing
is believing. When you see yourself take these steps, it is easier to
believe that the Great Turning is happening.

TRY THIS:
IDENTIFYING YOUR GOALS AND RESOURCES

This process works well when you team up with someone else, taking turns to interview and support each other.

1. If you knew you could not fail, what would you most want to do for the healing of our world?
2. What specific goal or project could you realistically aim to achieve in the next twelve months that would contribute to this?
3. What resources, inner and outer, do you have that will help you do this?

    Inner resources include specific strengths, qualities, and experience, as well as the knowledge and skills you've acquired.

    External resources include relationships, contacts, and networks you can draw on, as well as material resources such as money, equipment, and places to work or recharge.
4. What resources, inner and external, will you need to acquire? What might you need to learn, develop, or obtain?
5. How might you stop yourself? What obstacles might you throw in the way?
6. How will you overcome these obstacles?
7. What step can you take in the next week, no matter how small — making a phone call, sending an email, or scheduling in some reflection time — that will move you toward this goal?

You can repeat and review this process regularly. When we dare to believe that what we hope for is possible, we can dare to act. As a declaration often attributed to Goethe proclaims:

> Until one is committed, there is hesitancy, the chance to draw back. Concerning all acts of initiative (and creation), there is one elementary truth, the ignorance of which kills countless ideas and splendid plans: that the moment one definitely commits oneself, then Providence moves too. All sorts of things occur to help one that would never otherwise have occurred. A whole stream of events issues from the decision, raising in one's favor all manner of unforeseen incidents and meetings and material assistance, which no man could have dreamed would have come his way. Whatever you can do, or dream you can do, begin it. Boldness has genius, power, and magic in it. Begin it now.[4]

CHAPTER ELEVEN

Building Support around You

A crucial factor in any process of change is the level of support it receives. By seeking out encouragement, aid, and good counsel, we create a more favorable context both for our projects and for ourselves. Doing so is especially important when we are facing difficult or hostile conditions. In this chapter we will look at how we can cultivate support at the following levels:

- the personal context of our habits and practices
- the face-to-face context of the people around us
- the cultural context of the society we are part of
- the ecospiritual context of our connectedness with all life

PERSONAL CONTEXT: OUR HABITS AND PRACTICES

A good question to start with is, "Does the way I live my life support the changes I want to bring about?" Athletes selected for the Olympics are likely to train for years leading up to the event. Their choices about what they eat and drink and when they go bed are informed by their desire to bring out their best performance. Drawing on advanced methods of sports psychology, they may also use visualization and other practices to strengthen their motivation and sharpen their focus. If we recognize that we are living at a crucial point in human history, when our actions and choices will have consequences lasting thousands of years, is what we do any less important than an Olympic contest?

How we think about the value of what we do is crucial. If we don't see our role as important, we are less likely to take the steps required to function at our best. What helps us recognize our contribution to the Great Turning as significant enough to be worth taking seriously? The collaborative view of power, explored in chapter 6, certainly makes a difference, since our understanding of emergence helps us appreciate the hidden power of all our choices and actions. The Great Turning requires mass participation, and each of us has a role to play. But do we see our role as important enough to be worth supporting? This is a choice we can make. We can *choose* to give significance to our gift of Active Hope. There are practices that help us do this.

On the last afternoon of a two-week intensive workshop, Joanna was out walking and met a young monk from the retreat center hosting the event. "Well," he said, "I expect now on your last day you'll be giving people vows." Joanna told him that wasn't something she did. "Pity," he said. "I find, in my own life, vows so very helpful, because they channel my energy to do what I really want to do."

Continuing on her walk, Joanna looked at her hand and thought that if we were to have vows, they should not number more than the fingers and thumb of one hand. Almost immediately, the following five vows came to her:

I vow to myself and to each of you:

To commit myself daily to the healing of our world
and the welfare of all beings.

To live on Earth more lightly and less violently
in the food, products, and energy I consume.

To draw strength and guidance from the living Earth,
the ancestors, the future generations,
and my brothers and sisters of all species.

To support others in our work for the world
and to ask for help when I need it.

To pursue a daily practice
that clarifies my mind, strengthens my heart,
and supports me in observing these vows.

When the workshop participants were asked what they thought, "Oh, yes!" was their enthusiastic reply. With the workshop ending, they would soon be scattered far and wide; making these vows to one another and to themselves deepened their sense of being linked as a community. The words "I vow to myself and to each of you" calls to mind those we feel are with us as allies.

We need to choose terms that ring true for us. Rather than using the word vows, we can, if we prefer, call them "commitments" or "statements of intention." They offer an anchor point reminding us, again and again, of the purposes we hold dear and the behaviors that support us in serving them.

A group's declaration of intent gives tangible form to the shared desires of its members, providing a powerful rallying call. The five vows are an example of this. Now used by many people, they bring a heartening sense of belonging to a growing global fellowship of intention.

A practice is a habit we have chosen. It is something we have agreed to make a regular feature of our life. Habits develop momentum because the more we repeat them, the more ingrained they become. There are many practices that can support our intention to act for our world. Whether it be meditating, spending time in nature, taking daily vows, expressing ourselves creatively, or doing anything else we feel strengthened by, each nourishing activity becomes an ally adding to our context of support.

The fourth vow is to support each other in our work for the world, and to ask for help when we need it. This takes us into the second level of context — that involving the people around us.

Face-to-Face Context: The People around Us

Alan, a workshop participant, didn't like to ask for help. "My fear," he said, "is that if I ask for help, people will know I lack the ability to do the task myself. I'd be exposing the fact that I'm not as capable as I'd like them to think I am. That leaves me feeling deficient." In a society that divides people into winners and losers, or into those who cope and those who cannot, asking for help can feel like an admission of weakness.

What would happen to a football team if players thought they should be able to cope by themselves and so never passed the ball? The Great Turning is like a team sport; it is a collaborative process. There are times when we need to pass the ball, to call in the assistance of others, and times when we can offer our support too.

When we move from struggling by ourselves to acting as part of a network, we experience the shift in power expressed by the phrase "I can't, we can." Since looking for ways to develop synergy and co-intelligence is part of the Great Turning, the very process of seeking support is a positive step for change. One tool to help identify and amplify the help we receive is the support map. Here is a guide to creating one:

TRY THIS: CREATING A SUPPORT MAP

1. Start by placing your name in the center of a piece of paper. Around it, write the names of the people who are significant in your life.

2. Draw arrows to represent flows of support, with the arrows going toward your name for the support you receive and away from you for the support you offer. The thickness of the arrow reflects the strength of the support (see Fig. 11).

3. Once you've drawn your map, ask yourself how satisfied you are with the flows of support you receive and offer. Do you feel well sustained? If not, how could you invite in more of what you need?

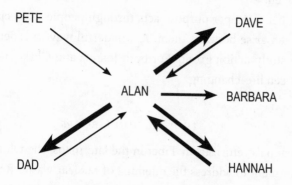

Figure 11. Alan's support map showing
the flow of giving and receiving.

When Alan looked at his support map, he was aware of how much better he was at offering support than he was at receiving it.

Apart from Hannah, his wife, there were few people he felt supported by, even though he knew his friends Pete and Dave would offer more if he'd let them. Because Alan had been so busy recently, he'd lost track of many old friends. He realized that instead of struggling on alone, he could ask for help, which would help him renew his friendships and make him more effective.

We can also use this mapping process for a specific project, putting the project's name in the center of the paper instead of our own. When you look at the people currently involved, and spot gaps or see that you are relying too much on yourself, you can start to think about who else to recruit. Each project has a life of its own, so it can be interesting to ask, "Through whom does this project want to act?" This question opens us to a more collaborative view. Rather than thinking in terms of "my project" or "their project," we can think of ourselves as part of a team recruited by a vision that wants to happen.

When a deeper purpose acts through people, a special kind of bond can arise between them. A wonderful way to experience this is in a study-action group. For both Joanna and Chris, such groups have been life-changing.

STUDY-ACTION GROUPS

On Joanna's return from Tibet in the late 1980s, she felt a renewed commitment to address the dilemma of nuclear waste. Recognizing the need both to learn more about the subject and to draw in support, she invited a dozen friends to join her in addressing the disposal of radioactive materials. From study groups in the 1970s, she recognized the benefits of adding an action element, in which the group applies what they learn to initiating a change in the world. This shared practical focus heightens energy, trust, and mutual respect in the group.

The group met monthly, and its work had three main strands,

which they called "the three S's": study, strategy, and mutual support. For the study strand, members took turns researching and teaching the others about particular areas, such as the physics of radiation, its biological effects, or the amounts of waste created by nuclear power and weapons production. The strategy side involved taking practical steps based on what they were finding out together. They gave talks in schools, organized petitions, and produced written materials.

Much of the subject matter was deeply disturbing. There were times when they needed to express the grief and anger they felt. That's why the third strand, mutual support, was so important, since it made room for the group's emotional responses and helped sustain the motivation and courage to keep going.

During the six years the group met, they created a training for themselves that equipped them to offer testimony at public hearings, conduct public education events, produce publications, and create a code of ethics on the care of radioactive materials. The three strands of study, strategy, and mutual support worked together to make the group's work a treasured experience.

Inspired by Joanna's experience, Chris and friends set up a study-action group about the Great Turning. The first step was to invite interested people to hear more about the idea and find out what they were able to commit to. Everyone who came was keen to take part, and the group agreed to meet monthly for six sessions, then to review. Keeping the size to just a dozen people, so that the group retained a sense of intimacy, they embarked on a journey guided by the questions "What is the Great Turning?" and "How can we take part in it?" A deeply nourishing sense of fellowship evolved. The group lasted eighteen months before it came to a natural ending point.

Study-action groups are attractive because they can happen in our homes, they don't require a high level of expertise to set up, and they are enjoyable. The key ingredients needed are a few people sharing a desire to learn more about an issue and to respond to it plus plenty of curiosity, willingness, tasty snacks, and a place to meet.

The study-action model we've described is only one of many forms a support group can take. If we find a book inspiring, another option is to gather a group to read and discuss it together. Doing so gives us an opportunity to read at a deeper level, helping us to digest new information and apply it in our lives.

CULTURAL CONTEXT

In their groundbreaking study involving more than a hundred thousand survey responses and hundreds of focus groups, social psychologists Paul Ray and Sherry Ruth Anderson describe the growth of a new subculture committed to ecological values, social justice, and holistic perspectives. Extrapolating their findings, they estimate that tens of millions of these "cultural creatives" are leaving behind the old story of Business as Usual and creating something new:

> When tens of millions of people make such choices in the space of a few decades, we are witnessing not simply a mass of personal departures but an exodus at the level of culture itself.[1]

This is the Great Turning. Yet it is not always easy to see, and as a result people often feel alone in their concern for the world. When reading mainstream newspapers and magazines, watching corporate-controlled television, or walking down a busy shopping street, we can have trouble finding evidence that others have noticed the planetary emergency we face. How can we cultivate a more supportive context at the level of our culture and society?

A major factor influencing our decisions is what we believe others around us are doing. Research shows that people are more likely to reduce their energy consumption when they know their neighbors are doing so too.[2] Each of us has a reference group of those we compare ourselves to in determining what is normal or appropriate behavior. We also feature in other people's reference groups, so when they see us taking steps to live more sustainably, they are more likely to take these steps too.

The recognition of the power of example at a local level has led to a kind of community organizing that now involves hundreds of thousands of people in the United States. Developed through decades of action research, the "cool communities" campaign on carbon reduction brings together people from the same street or block in small "eco-teams" to bring about measurable reductions in their carbon footprint.[3]

One finding of the cool communities program is that in spite of initial skepticism about people's willingness to work with their neighbors on developing sustainable lifestyles, once the process got started, it developed a momentum of its own. As David Gershon, who developed this approach, describes:

> I started with the point of view of thinking people won't want to disturb their neighbors, they'll be rejected. In New York City, where I live, people said, "We don't talk to our neighbors and we're happy about that. We like our individuality." This is not actually the case and it is a paradox. It is not so much that people don't want to know their neighbors, it is that they don't know how to connect with the people living next door and build community. As a result, we struggle as isolated and alienated individuals.
>
> The resistance of "I don't know my neighbors, we've never done anything like this, I'm afraid I'll be rejected" is something we've experienced everywhere we've worked. But

once we get people through this using the organizing tools we provide, they come out the other side feeling incredibly excited to have that connection. Again and again, people say that what they like most about the program is getting to know their neighbors.[4]

When volunteers were recruited, trained, and supported to knock on the doors of their neighbors — inviting them to join small local groups making lifestyle changes to reduce their carbon footprint — the participation rate was over 40 percent. The level of concern, as well as the willingness to become involved, was much higher than was anticipated from initial appearances. The desire to take part in the healing of our world seems to be just below the surface, waiting for an opportunity and outlet for expression.

Whenever we bring the desire for the world's healing out into the open, whether through our individual actions or through the groups we are part of, we help others do this too. The power of example is contagious. This is how cultures change.

ECOSPIRITUAL CONTEXT:
OUR CONNECTEDNESS WITH ALL LIFE

Recent research gives strong support to something we know from our own experience: contact with the natural environment can be powerfully restorative to our well-being.[5] Prisoners who can look out of their cells get sick less often, and patients in hospitals recover more quickly when their view is of greenery rather than concrete. In developing a context that supports us in working for our world, we need to include contact with nature.

There is something more fundamental here than the feel-good factor of pleasant scenery. Particularly for those living in cities, it is easy to lose touch with the biological reality that we arise out of nature and are part of it. While the Haudenosaunee and other indigenous peoples recognize that our very survival depends on the healthy functioning of the natural world, it is only recently that we've gained a scientific understanding of how true this really is.

We wouldn't have the oxygen we breathe if it weren't for plant life and plankton. We wouldn't have the food we eat if it weren't for the rich living matrix of soil, plants, pollinating insects, and other forms of life. When we carry within us a deep appreciation of how our life is sustained by other living beings, we strengthen our desire to give back.

With the first three levels of context — the practices, the people, and the culture we're part of — we're referring to tangible behaviors and entities we can point to and that other people can observe. With this fourth level of context, we're describing an experience of connection that leaves us feeling held and supported even when there's nobody else around and nothing particular we're doing. We call this fourth context "ecospiritual" because it is about our felt relationship to wider dimensions of reality.

Each of us has an inner map marking the realms we regard as supremely important or sacred, purposes we deem worth following, and sources we trust for renewal and guidance. In the map of reality that accompanies the Business as Usual story, money is what matters most; anything that gets in the way of short-term profiteering becomes an unfortunate casualty. On this map, the route to gaining support is through acquiring the money needed to pay for it. This map is taking us over the edge of a cliff.

The third dimension of the Great Turning involves a shift in consciousness. We can think of this shift as changing our map to one that puts the healing of our world at the very center of things. On this map, our community is all of life. So we know the trees, the insects, and birds as our kith and kin, as our extended family, as parts of our larger, ecological self. With this map of reality, our ecospiritual context is populated with allies. The desire that life continue is larger than we are, and when our actions are guided by this desire, we can imagine around us the cheering of all those sharing our aims: the ancestors, the future beings, the natural world itself. When we're feeling alone, discouraged, or desperate, we can turn to any of these for support.

If we're not accustomed to seeking solace from the natural world, a good place to start is by casting our mind back to our fondest memories of times spent in nature. Were there any special places where we felt especially at peace or that we particularly loved to visit? Drawing on our memories and imagination, we can mentally return to these places and recall the feeling of receiving from nature; in reliving this experience, we receive again. Even better is to find a special place in nature where we can go and make contact. We can think of this as similar to visiting an old friend or mentor. But can a place really speak to us? Try the following exercise and see what happens.

TRY THIS:
FINDING A LISTENING POST IN NATURE

Is there a place where you feel more connected to the web of life? It can be either somewhere you go physically or somewhere in your imagination. Each time you go there, make yourself comfortable. Think of yourself plugging in to a root system that can draw up insights and inspiration as well as other nutrients. To receive guidance, all you need to do is ask for it, and then listen.

CHAPTER TWELVE

Maintaining Energy and Enthusiasm

When we catch the spark of heartfelt activism for our world, that inner fire can be a remarkable source of energy. However, it also brings with it the risk of burnout. How can we remain fired up for any length of time without being driven to exhaustion? In this chapter we look at how to keep inspiration fresh by making what we do more enjoyable and by keeping personal sustainability right at the heart of what we do.

With our world in crisis, it might seem a bit indulgent to be considering our own enjoyment. With so many pressing issues to address, shouldn't we brush aside concerns about personal gratification? Yet there is a strategic value to making what we do rewarding, and it goes further than just preventing burnout. Although many millions of people are already involved in the Great Turning, the movement needs to grow, and the attractiveness of participation grows when it is recognized as a path to deepened aliveness and a more satisfying way of life. Here are five strategies that help.

- Recognize enthusiasm as a valuable renewable resource.
- Broaden our definition of activism.
- Follow the inner compass of our deep gladness.
- Redefine what it means to have a good life.
- See success with new eyes and savor it.

RECOGNIZE ENTHUSIASM AS A
VALUABLE RENEWABLE RESOURCE

Each year, erosion from unsustainable agriculture robs our world of as much farmland as could cover the whole of Kentucky. Similarly, when we push ourselves too hard or are worn down by chronic exposure to harsh conditions, our enthusiasm, like topsoil, can begin to erode.

In responding to the problems of our world, we do need to stretch ourselves and face adversities. The problem is that stretching too far and for too long brings with it the risk of burnout. This state of physical and emotional exhaustion is a form of overshoot and collapse; it is caused by long-term exposure to high levels of stress along with insufficient time and nourishment for renewal. Jenny, who'd worked for many years in a campaigning organization, described what it felt like:

I used to love the work I did. I used to enjoy giving talks and engaging with people. But I reached the point where I felt sick of everything. I had worked too hard for too long, and I didn't have anything left to give.

When athletes want to improve their performance, they expect to push beyond their comfort zones. Through the well-established principle of interval training, they alternate periods of increased effort with pauses for renewal. A similar principle applies in yoga when a stretch extends briefly beyond what is comfortable and then draws back. When we keep pushing we risk harming ourselves. To develop forms of activism we can sustain for decades, we need to address our requirements for renewal. If we are to create an approach to activism that we will want to stick with over a lifetime and that others are drawn to as well, then we need to look at what feeds our enthusiasm too.

Sustainable agriculture reveals how valuable a resource healthy soil is. Finding ways to nourish, renew, and restore soil is a key to long-term productivity. It is similar with our enthusiasm: if we see it as valuable, then we become more interested in how we can nourish, renew, and restore this precious resource.

An image of a boat floating on water provides a starting point for mapping out the factors influencing our ability and willingness to keep going (see Fig. 12). The water level represents our inner reserves of energy and enthusiasm, while hitting a problem like burnout is like crashing into a rock. Draining factors are shown as downward arrows that lower the water level and increase our likelihood of hitting rocks. Nourishing factors that replenish and strengthen us are mapped as arrows pushing the water level up. For example, when we feel we're making progress with our projects, our morale is boosted, raising the water level. Each time we feel discouraged, whether by setbacks, arguments, or the experience of powerlessness, the water level drops. So to strengthen our resilience, we need to pay attention to all the factors that sustain us.

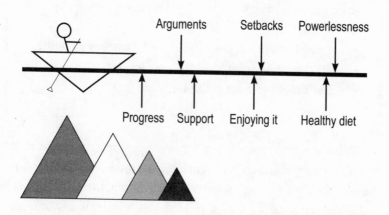

Figure 12. Mapping factors influencing our energy and enthusiasm

If we experience too much discouragement and too few "up-ward arrows," then we are in danger of reaching such a low ebb that we may wonder what the point is and think about giving up. When we lose the will, energy, and enthusiasm to continue, we're hitting the rock of burnout.

With the worsening condition of our world, the slow pace of progress, and the enormous resistance to tackling issues, protecting our enthusiasm has become especially important. Building support around us, as discussed in the previous chapter, plays a central role here, but it is only one of many potential "upward arrows." Once we recognize the value of enthusiasm, we start searching for ways to make what we do more satisfying. The following open sentences invite this exploration.

TRY THIS: OPEN SENTENCES ON
MAINTAINING ENERGY AND ENTHUSIASM

These open sentences can be used when journaling, in con-versation with friends, or within a group. They work well in conjunction with the water level mapping process.

- Things that drain, demoralize, or exhaust me include...
- What nourishes and energizes me is...
- The times I'm most enthusiastic are when...

What might happen if we applied open sentences like these when planning meetings or events? Many public meetings follow the old model of having an active speaker at the front of the room and a passive audience sitting in rows, with little, if any, interac-tion. Sometimes these meetings can be informative and inspiring; they can also be boring and can induce passivity. The water level diagram can be used to map out factors that make the difference. How can we push up the water level of enthusiasm in meetings so that people look forward to coming rather than just showing up out of duty?

A sustainability group in Frome, England, had a meeting every month, often with a speaker or a film followed by a discussion. Their meetings became much more popular when they started the evening by sitting down together and eating food they'd brought to share. By having time and opportunity to talk with each other, they fed the friendships and sense of community that made them look forward to coming. Conversations while eating have led to a sprouting of collaborative projects and activities that have transformed the local community.

Broaden Our Definition of Activism

What is the opposite of an activist? Is it someone who is passive? If so, it seems strange that the term *activist* should be reserved for just a few of us rather than being an identity we all take pride in or aspire to. The practice of Active Hope involves being an activist for what we hope for in the world. We're using the term *activist* here to mean anyone who is active for a purpose bigger than personal gain.

The three dimensions of the Great Turning offer a structure that extends the range of activism beyond the important work of campaigning and protest. Whenever we act from bodhichitta, the desire that all life be well, we are being an activist. This includes all endeavors to build a sustainable culture, along with everything that promotes the shift in consciousness and perception supporting this. Having a larger map of activism encourages us to move more freely between these different dimensions, as well as to combine them in ways that empower us. It is possible to overextend ourselves in any of these dimensions, and it can be refreshing to switch track, to move from one area to another, when we are getting worn down.

"Our activism is through our publishing," say Tim and Maddy Harland, who for more than twenty years have produced *Permaculture* magazine. "Our activism is through growing things," say Manu Song and Edi Hamilton, founders of a community agriculture project. Taking part in the Great Turning doesn't have to mean suddenly changing jobs or giving up our other interests. Rather, it means applying our skills, experience, networks, enthusiasm, and temperament to the healing of our world. A participant in an online discussion organized by Transition U.S. said:

> The three types of action to achieve the Great Turning is a very helpful structure.... I am by nature better geared to one kind of this work than another and it is okay to apply myself where I work best.

FOLLOW THE INNER COMPASS OF OUR DEEP GLADNESS

While there may be periods when we feel ground down or discouraged, there are also times when activism is hugely satisfying, stimulating, and enjoyable. By becoming interested in what makes this so, we can identify what we want to focus on. The flip side of this is that when we feel ourselves going sour inside, experiencing resentment and a loss of our spark, it is worth pausing and reflecting on the choices we can make to restore our enthusiasm. Our degree of enthusiasm can act as a guide, like an inner compass, that helps us steer toward the sort of activity we'll want to stick with in the long term.

We are more effective when acting from our strengths and enthusiasm. That is where the Great Turning can happen through us most powerfully. This is a big shift away from the idea that there is one right way forward that we should all follow. Rather, it suggests that each of us needs to find our place of greatest fit. Author and minister Frederick Buechner describes this as where "our deep gladness and the world's deep need meet."[1] When we find this convergence, the Great Turning works through us in a way uniquely ours.

REDEFINE WHAT IT MEANS TO HAVE A GOOD LIFE

The view of a satisfying life presented by glossy magazines and advertisements involves luxury and leisure, illustrated by images of people sunbathing by swimming pools and being served martinis. The scientific research on happiness shows this to be a long way from what really makes life satisfying. Psychologist Mihaly Csikszentmihalyi, in his classic book *Flow: The Psychology of Happiness*, writes:

> The best moments usually occur when a person's body or mind is stretched to its limits in a voluntary effort to accomplish something difficult and worthwhile.[2]

Luxury doesn't challenge and stretch us in a way that leads to satisfaction. But activism does in a number of ways. First, when we act in alignment with our deepest values, we experience an inner sense of rightness behind what we do. Second, when we apply ourselves to facing a challenge in a way that absorbs our attention, we are more likely to go into the flow states that psychologists like Csikszentmihalyi have linked so strongly to life satisfaction.

To go into this kind of flow state, we want to face a challenge difficult enough to absorb us but not so difficult that we feel defeated. When we use our strengths and enthusiasms, we're more likely to enter the nourishing state of absorption where we lose all track of time. This creates a self-reinforcing spiral, where the more we act from our strengths the more we go into flow, and the more we become absorbed by an activity, the better we get at it. We gain even more satisfaction when "virtuous cycles" like this contribute to our world.

If we believe the research findings rather than the advertising industry, activism offers a more reliable path to a satisfying life than consumerism. Unfortunately, for both our world and our collective mood, this is not yet the dominant view. However, an international movement committed to redefining what it means to have a good life is growing.[3] In England, Chris set up the Bristol Happiness Lectures, a series of annual talks that have attracted hundreds of people each year and been watched by many more on YouTube.[4] One year the theme was "happiness and sustainability." The title of Chris's talk was "How Facing Bad News about the World Can Make You Happier."

At first sight, people may scratch their heads at this title and ask, "Are you serious?" The conventional view is that awareness of world problems is a threat to happiness and, as a result, it is resisted. At issue here are two different understandings of what good mood is based on; one aims for a happy picture, and the other engages in a satisfying process.

The happy-picture approach works along the lines of "If only I had _____ then I'd be happy," happiness here being linked to having the right things. The usual list of desired items includes money, success, and good looks, plus whatever consumer items are most in fashion at the time. If we don't have the right things or look the right way, then our life is not a "happy picture." It is easy to feel deficient when measuring ourselves against this manufactured stereotype; our resultant dissatisfaction is a strong driver of consumerism.

One thing you don't find in a happy picture is bad news. Keeping the picture smiley and upbeat involves resisting sources of gloom, so unwelcome features of reality get airbrushed out of view and screened out of conversation. This approach leaves us completely unprepared when we finally get it that we are facing a crisis.

A satisfying process is more like a good story that has both ups and downs. There is no need to hide from bad news here; indeed, it may be the very thing that provokes us to act in a way that makes our life more satisfying. When we rise to a challenge, our strengths are activated and our sense of purpose switched on. There is no guarantee we will succeed in bringing about the changes we hope for, but the process of giving our full attention and effort draws out our aliveness. This is what Active Hope is all about; when we live this way, the boredom and emptiness so prevalent in modern society simply disappear.

Someone whose story illustrates the contrast between these two approaches to the good life is John Robbins. At the age of twenty, his life was the American dream come true. His father and uncle had set up the largest ice-cream business in history, and John was being groomed to become the next CEO. Something in this happy picture didn't feel right, though. The company's advertising slogan, "we make people happy," didn't ring true to John. While ice cream and smiles might seem to go together, the consequence of reinforcing this pairing is an increase in obesity and heart disease. What was good for making money wasn't good for people's health. In his book *The New Good Life*, John describes his dilemma:

> An ice cream cone never killed anyone, but the more ice cream people eat the more likely they are to develop health problems, and the company naturally wanted to sell as much ice cream as possible.

John felt not only that this obsession with money was wrong, but also that it took people away from the things that make life most worthwhile. Describing the pull of a path he found more attractive, he wrote:

> I felt called to a different way of life, one whose purpose wasn't focused on making the most money but on making the

most difference.... If I were to refuse that call, I might end up
rich, but I would surely end up untrue to myself and unhappy.
To live against our innermost values can make us sick. It also
can lead to disingenuous, counterfeit, or artificial lives.[5]

A truly satisfying process is one we have our heart in; for John,
life as a multimillionaire executive didn't offer this. At the age of
twenty-one, he turned his back on the vast financial wealth that
could have been his. He washed dishes and did other part-time work
to support himself through college. In 1969 he and his wife, Deo,
went to live in a tiny one-room log cabin they built on an island in
Canada. For the next ten years, they lived a simple life, growing
much of their own food and thriving on less than a thousand dollars between them each year. Describing the contrast to the world
of money he had grown up in, he wrote:

> Both Deo and I wanted to know if something else was pos-
> sible and might even be more fulfilling...something in our
> bones told us that humanity was on a collision course with
> tragedy, and we felt compelled to step out of the rat race so we
> could more authentically step into our lives.[6]

Some years later, John went on to write the million-copy best-
seller *Diet for a New America*, in which he explores the links between
food, health, and our environment.[7] The income from book sales
didn't deflect John and Deo from their simple life; they'd discovered something on that Canadian island that was both profoundly
fulfilling and deeply important to them. It is a game any of us can
play, and it has the potential to enrich our lives and transform our
world. Here's how John describes it:

> The object of the game is to see how much you can lower your
> spending while raising your quality of life.[8]

If everyone lived as the average North American or European does, we'd need three to five planets like Earth to supply the resources and cope with the rubbish.[9] Because the link between happiness and consumerism has been so powerfully woven into our culture, the idea of "giving up" or "cutting back" is usually seen as grim and threatening. Yet, as John points out, the real losses come from consumerism. Bit by bit, we are losing our world. We are losing the forests, the fish, the bees; we are wiping out whole species. We are losing the richness of community and much of what makes life meaningful. We are now on the brink of losing the biological support systems we need to survive.

Through the game of learning to live well with less, we stand to gain. We stand to increase our resilience at a time of financial uncertainty, reducing the anxiety over how we'll manage when money is short or loses its value. This game played well leads to happier, more fulfilling lives.

SEE SUCCESS WITH NEW EYES

While having our heart in what we do is an essential part of what makes life satisfying, it isn't enough. Repeated failure, frustration, and lack of progress can leave us wondering whether we're wasting our time. It is difficult to stick to a path if we don't see it going anywhere. So the way we understand and experience success affects our willingness to keep going.

The models of success we're likely to have been given generally take us in the wrong direction. In the story of Business as Usual, success is measured in terms of wealth, fame, or position. A company making massive profits is regarded as successful, even when its ways of doing this harm its employees and our world. People are judged as successful simply because they have managed to acquire a vastly larger share of the world's resources than they could ever need — at a time when hundreds of millions starve. It is the very hunger for this type of success that leads us, collectively, to plunder our planet.

With the consciousness shift of the Great Turning, we recognize ourselves as intimately connected with all life, like a cell within a larger body. To call an individual cell "successful" while the larger body sickens or dies is complete nonsense. If we are to survive as a civilization, we need the intelligence to define success as that which contributes to the well-being of our larger body, the web of life. Commercial success is easy to count, but how do we count the success of contributing to planetary well-being? Do we experience this success often? And if not, what is getting in the way?

TRY THIS: REFLECTING ON SUCCESS

Taking your definition of success as that which contributes to the well-being of our world, how often do you feel you are succeeding?

We experience success when we reach a goal that is significant to us. But what if our goal is the elimination of poverty or the transition to a low-carbon economy? If the change we want doesn't happen in our lifetime, does that mean we will never experience success? For the encouraging boost we get when we know we're moving forward, we need to find markers of progress we can spot more easily and often. What helps here is making the distinction between eventual goals and intermediate ones.

The progressive brainstorming process described in chapter 9 began with longer-range, eventual goals. These are the things we would really like to see happen, even if we can't immediately see how they will come about. We take one of these eventual goals and list some of the conditions needed to bring it about. So if our goal is the elimination of poverty, we would need to have in place widespread political will, new taxation policies, redistribution of resources, and the like. Then, taking one of these, we ask, "What would be needed for this?" Each stage moves us closer to our present situation. Before long, we're identifying steps that are within our reach, such as eating lower in the food chain or setting up a study-action group on world hunger.

For any goal we choose to pursue, we track back in time to identify intermediate steps. Each time we take a step like this, we are succeeding. Instead of rushing on immediately to the next task, we can take a moment to savor these mini-victories. The following open sentence is a useful prompt for this process.

TRY THIS: SAVORING SUCCESS EVERY DAY

A recent step I've taken that I feel good about is...

There are steps we take that often don't get counted, like the choice of where to place our attention. Just noticing that things are seriously amiss is a step on the journey. If we care enough to want to do something, that is also a significant mini-victory. Just to show up with bodhichitta is a success.

In a society that views success in competitive terms, it is usually only those recognized as "winners" who are applauded. We need to learn the skill of encouraging and applauding ourselves. We can reinforce our appreciation of the steps we take by imagining the support of the ancestors, the future beings, and the more-than-human world. When we develop our receptivity, we will sense them cheering us on. If we form a study-action group or build support in other ways, we can take time to do this for each other, noticing and appreciating what we're doing well.

When we reflect on past successes, we can ask, "What strengths in me helped me do that?" Naming our strengths makes them more available to us. However, the challenges we face demand of us more commitment, endurance, and courage than we could ever dredge up out of our individual supply. That is why we need to make the essential shift of seeing with new eyes — it takes the process of strength recognition to a new level, that of the larger web of life. Just as we can identify with the suffering of other beings in this web, so too can we identify with their successes and draw on their strengths. There is an ancient Buddhist meditation that helps us do this. It is called "the Great Ball of Merit" and it is excellent training for the moral imagination:

TRY THIS: THE GREAT BALL OF MERIT

Relax and close your eyes, relax into your breathing... Open your awareness to the fellow beings who share with you this planet-time...in this room...this neighborhood... this town. Open to all those in this country and in other lands...Let your awareness encompass all beings living now in our world.

Opening now to all time, let your awareness encompass all beings who have ever lived...of all races and creeds and walks of life, rich and poor, kings and beggars, saints and sinners...Like successive mountain ranges, the vast vistas of these fellow beings present themselves to your mind's eye.

Now open to the knowledge that in each of these innumerable lives some act of merit was performed. No matter how stunted or deprived the life, there was at the very least one gesture of kindness, one gift of love, or one act of valor or self-sacrifice...on the battlefield or in the work-place, hospital or home...From each of these beings in their endless multitudes arose actions of courage, kindness, of teaching and healing...Let yourself see these manifold, immeasurable acts of merit.

Now imagine that you can sweep together these acts of merit. Sweep them into a pile in front of you. Use your hands...pile them up...pile them into a heap, viewing it with gladness and gratitude. Now pat them into a ball. It is the Great Ball of Merit. Hold it now and weigh it in your hands...Rejoice in it, knowing that no act of goodness is ever lost. It remains ever and always a present resource...a means for the transformation of life...So now, with jubilation and thanksgiving, you turn that great ball, turn it over...over...into the healing of our world.

The more we practice this meditation, the more familiar we become with the process of drawing strengths from outside our narrow self. Knowing about the Great Ball of Merit can also change the way we think about our own actions. Each time we do something, no matter how small, that is guided by bodhichitta and contributes to our world, we know we are adding to this abundance.

CHAPTER THIRTEEN

Strengthened by Uncertainty

In his study of environmental factors threatening the viability of our civilization, Jared Diamond identifies a dozen issues that are "like time bombs."[1] Any of these, including climate change, peak oil, water scarcity, overpopulation, habitat destruction, loss of topsoil, and rising toxin levels, could trigger the collapse of our society. In combination, their impact is even more devastating. As these perils worsen, along with ever-increasing wars and the continued production of weapons of mass destruction, the Great Unraveling becomes more difficult to ignore. Many of us are left feeling so uncertain about the future that we wonder whether we will make it.

In the story of Business as Usual, alarm and dread over these conditions are far from welcome. To address all these issues, we would have to change our way of living, our systems of accounting, our pattern of energy consumption, our modes of transport, and the entire basis of our industrial-growth economy. Can we justify the costs and upheaval of all this if we can't prove beyond a doubt that these measures are necessary and absolutely sure to solve our problems? When we're attached to the old way of doing things, uncertainty is used to support the "Big No" to any suggestion that we need to change our way of life.

The Great Turning begins with a different view. When we face the mess we are in, we *know* the future is uncertain. That is an unavoidable feature of our times. But what we do with this uncertainty is a matter of choice. In this chapter, we explore how our very not knowing can enliven us; by making friends with uncertainty, we can become strengthened by the gifts it has to offer.

HOW WE LOOK AT UNCERTAINTY

If we take action only when we are reasonably sure of success, uncertainty can be paralyzing. In tackling climate change, for example, we can't be sure we haven't already passed a tipping point that sets us on track for a doomsday scenario. The sense that our world might be coming to an end is already leading many people to give up, to become cynical and drained of purpose. After all, what is the point of making an effort to improve things if we believe catastrophe is inevitable? If we are not to be blocked by the part of us that wonders whether we're already too late, we need a different way of relating to the challenging uncertainties of our time.

In Chris's addiction work, every year some clients he knew well died from their alcohol and drug use, while others grew stronger in their recovery. When he saw new clients, he never knew which way they would go. It was a good sign when they felt this same uncertainty too. If they were certain things would go well, there was a danger of complacency. On the other hand, if they saw themselves as hopeless cases, their belief that a downward spiral was inevitable led them to give up, creating a self-fulfilling prophecy. Thank goodness for uncertainty. When we know the future isn't yet decided, there is room for us to play a role in influencing what happens.

When we fall in love or start out in a career, can we be certain it will work out well? When contractions herald the birth of new life, is a safe delivery, or even the baby's survival, guaranteed? Life, in its richness and mystery, never offers guarantees of success. We don't let that stop us. Indeed, our awareness that the outcome is uncertain is what prompts us to prepare; it calls us to attention. Neither complacent optimism nor resigned pessimism has power to motivate us; they don't generate a hunger for learning or provoke our best response.

UNCERTAINTY ADDS MYSTERY AND ADVENTURE

What is it that keeps people's eyes glued to the ball when watching a sport? What impels us to turn the page when reading a novel? It is our not knowing what's going to happen yet our wanting to. If we already knew what was going to happen next, what would keep us from falling asleep? Our lives get boring when they are too predictable. We can feel like we are just going through the motions. But notice the times when our heart quickens, when we snap awake with our full attention aroused. When do those moments occur? Here is one from Chris's life:

> *After nearly ten years of medical training, I'd recently resigned and was now out of a job. It felt like a life-or-death decision, since just a few months before, when recovering from a working week of 112 hours, I'd fallen asleep while driving and had totaled my car. I could easily have been killed, or have killed someone else. And now I didn't know what I was going to do, where I was going to live, or how I was going to support myself. I just knew, deep in my bones, that I had to get out.*
>
> *My legs were wobbly with fear, my knees like jelly. I had gone to sit in the hills of Wales, to have contact with nature and to ask for help. As I sat there, watching the clouds and the grass and the insects, I burst out laughing. I'd been hit by a moment of clarity, and it seemed funny. My problem and my fear was that I didn't know what was going to happen. Yet it was this very not knowing that made for mystery in life. I didn't know what lay around the corner in time; opening to the mystery and adventure of this left me feeling not fear but excitement.*

If we have spent decades building a life in Business as Usual and our sense of security is linked to this, then moving into the uncharted territory of a different story is likely to bring up fear. Being too attached to familiarity can make uncertainty feel as scary as the outside world is for an agoraphobic. That is why it is so easy to get stuck in what's familiar, even when we know this isn't good for us or for our world.

Since stepping into new ground involves frequent encounters with not knowing, we need to make friends with this feeling. It will be a companion on our journey.

UNCERTAINTY BRINGS US INTO THE PRESENT

The elegant poise of a martial artist embodies a state of readiness. At any moment an attack may come, a block may be needed, a swift move required. Who will strike? Where and when? Not knowing brings your attention fully into the present. Being anywhere else means you end up on the floor. Times of crisis have a similar effect: they wake us up and engage our full attention.

Bringing ourselves into the present moment doesn't mean we lose connection with the past or future. We are shaped by our history; it is part of who we are. What we add is intentionality. This choice-making is our bridge to the future, as each intention represents a preference for the kind of world we want. Our intentionality endows the present moment with direction.

When Joanna was in Tibet, she received an important teaching about the power of intention from watching the monks rebuild the monastery of Khampagar. Once a major center of Tibetan Buddhist culture and learning, it had been destroyed by the Red Guards during the Chinese Cultural Revolution. A shift to a more relaxed occupation policy had allowed reconstruction to begin. This policy, however, could be reversed at any moment; there was no guarantee that the monastery, once rebuilt, would not be destroyed again.

That didn't stop the monks. They faced the uncertainty by bringing to it their intention. They assumed that since you cannot know, you simply proceed. You do what you have to do. You put one stone on top of another and another on top of that. If the stones are knocked down, you begin again, because if you don't, nothing will be built. You persist. In the long run, it is persistence that shapes the future.

BODHICHITTA

With the uncertainties we face, we need a strength of intention similar to that of those Tibetan monks. If we take bodhichitta — the desire for the welfare of all beings — as our foundation stone, then that is what we can count on, whatever else is happening. Bodhichitta is grounded in our conscious connectedness with all life. So this is our starting point. It is what we build on. Moving around the spiral of the Work That Reconnects helps us strengthen this connectedness, helps us open to and trust it more. Each time we go around the spiral, we reinforce our bodhichitta. In a time of uncertainty, it can be the one thing we are sure of.

In the Buddhist tradition, bodhichitta is seen as something very precious, something to treasure and protect. We can think of it as a flame in our hearts and minds that guides us and shines through our actions. The bodhisattvas, the hero figures of the Buddhist tradition, have such strong bodhichitta that even when they reach the gates of nirvana, having earned the right to disappear into eternal bliss, they turn around every time and choose to come back. They choose to return to samsara, this realm of suffering, because their bodhichitta calls them to serve life on Earth and act for the welfare of all beings.

We can play with this image of the bodhisattva choosing to return to our world and use it as the starting point for a thought experiment. Trying out a different way of thinking about our situation is a powerful way of strengthening our resilience and creativity. The bodhisattva archetype is present in all religions and even all social movements. Whenever you act for the sake of life on Earth, you express the courageous compassion within you that we can think of as your bodhisattva self. This is part of who you are. You don't have to be a Buddhist or believe in reincarnation to benefit from the exercise described below. We invite you to try it and see where it takes you.

TRY THIS: THE BODHISATTVA PERSPECTIVE

The starting point for this process is to imagine yourself poised at the gateway into your present life. You are back before your birth into this lifetime of yours. For this incarnation, you will have an opportunity to take part in the great changes arising with the dawn of the third millennium; after many decades of growing danger, human civilization is bringing the world to a point of unparalleled peril and promise.

The challenges take many forms — the making and using of nuclear weapons, industrial technologies that poison and lay waste to whole ecosystems, billions of people sinking into poverty — but one thing is clear. A quantum leap in consciousness is required if life is to prevail on Earth. Hearing this, you decide to renew your commitment to life and reenter the fray by taking birth as a human living on Earth at this time, bringing with you everything you've ever learned about courage and community. This is a major decision. And it is a hard decision because there is no guarantee that you will remember why you came back and no assurance that you will succeed in your mission. Furthermore, you may well feel alone, because you probably won't even recognize the many other bodhisattvas who, like you, have chosen to be born into this time.

Take a moment to reflect on your willingness to take a human birth in so challenging a planet-time. It is your bodhichitta that calls you. Yet this is such a harsh time, and you are aware that you may be born into a life much touched by suffering.

Every human life is by necessity a particular life. You can't take birth as a generic human, but only as a unique human shaped by particular circumstances. So feel yourself stepping into these circumstances now. Imagine that you choose them in awareness of how they will help prepare you to serve the flourishing of life.

Step into the year of your birth. The timing of your birth allows you to be affected by particular conditions and events....

Step into the place of your birth. What country did you choose? Were you born in a town or a city, or on the land? Which parts of the Earth's body first greeted your eyes?

Which skin color and ethnicity did you select? And what socioeconomic conditions? Both the privileges and the privations resulting from these choices help prepare you for the work you are coming to do....

Into what faith tradition — or lack thereof — were you born this time? Religious stories and images from child-hood — or the very lack of these — influence how you see and search for your purpose....

Now here's an important choice: which gender did you adopt this time around? And which sexual preference?...

And as to your parents: what man did you choose to be your father? What woman your mother? This might mean your adoptive parents as well as your birth parents. Both the strengths and the weaknesses of your parents, both the loving care you received and the hurts you experienced, help prepare you for the work you are coming to do....

Are you an only child, or do you have siblings in this life? The companionship, the competition, or the loneliness that ensued from that choice will foster the unique blend of strengths you bring to your world....

What disabilities did you choose to take on this time? Challenges of body or mind can deepen your understanding of the difficulties and capacities of others.

Certain strengths and passions characterize this life of yours too. Which mental, physical, and spiritual powers and appetites did you choose for yourself in this planet-time?...

And last, imagining that you can for a moment see it clearly, what particular mission are you coming to perform?...

Each choice relates to your actual life and not to any fantasized alternative to it. What you're doing is seeing these choices from a more encompassing dimension of consciousness. It is as though you're remembering an important part of your identity that may have been hidden from view. With this process, you're becoming reacquainted with the bodhisattva within you. You can do this process as a personal reflection, writing in a journal or as a letter to yourself. If you are doing it with a friend or in a small group, you can take turns checking in with each other, describing your experience of this process and any insights, thoughts, or feelings it evokes.

As you become familiar with this exercise, you may wish to add or subtract topics for the bodhisattvas' report. A follow-up session can reflect on choices we made in the course of this lifetime, relating, for example, to educational endeavors, spiritual practices, central relationships, and vocational explorations and commitments. After participating in this process, a colleague wrote:

> I have been thinking a lot about the Bodhisattva's Choices. I found it very empowering. I consider myself an accountable person. Yet I'd never before systematically reviewed all the major circumstances in my life and celebrated them for bringing me to this time and place.

We are aware that the idea of our choosing our life conditions may be problematic for some people. The idea of taking responsibility for situations that have oppressed us can smack of blaming the victim. Our purpose, however, is to recognize that all life's experiences, even the harsh and limiting ones, can be seen as ennobling and enriching to our understanding and motivations to serve. Spiritual traditions affirm that true liberation arises when we can embrace the particulars of our lives and see that they are as right for us as if we had indeed chosen them.

FINDING THE PEARL OF ACTIVE HOPE

When Boris Cyrulnik was ten years old, he had to go into hiding. Living in France during the German occupation, he needed to stay invisible to survive. Because of their Jewish descent, other members of his family were taken to Auschwitz and killed. Boris's experience of extreme hardship left him with questions about what helps us find strength, what deepens our resilience. Working with abused children, child soldiers in Colombia, and survivors of genocide in

Rwanda, he became one of the world's leading psychologists addressing children's recovery from trauma. In his book *Resilience*, he writes:

> The pearl inside the oyster might be the emblem of resilience. When a grain of sand gets into an oyster and is so irritating that, in order to defend itself, the oyster has to secrete a nacreous substance, the defensive reaction produces a material that is hard, shiny and precious.[2]

We live at a time when the living body of our Earth is under attack and when the attacker is not an alien force but our own industrial-growth society. At the same time, an extraordinary recovery process is under way, a vital creative response we call the Great Turning. What helps us face the mess we're in is the knowledge that each of us has something significant to offer, a contribution to make. In rising to the challenge of playing our best role, we discover something precious that both enriches our lives and adds to the healing of our world. An oyster, in response to trauma, grows a pearl. We grow, and offer, our gift of Active Hope.

Notes

All websites accessed August/September 2011.

ACKNOWLEDGMENTS

Thich Nhat Hanh, *The Heart of Understanding: Commentaries on the Prajnaparamita Heart Sutra* (Berkeley, CA: Parallax Press, 1988), 3.

INTRODUCTION

1. In a 2002 global poll of 25,164 people from 175 countries, 67 percent thought global environmental conditions are getting worse. See http://netpulseglobalpoll.politicsonline.com/results/highlights.doc.
2. Nobel Prize–winning economist Joseph Stiglitz and colleague Linda Bilmes calculated that the United States has spent more than $3 trillion on the war in Iraq. See *The Three Trillion Dollar War* (New York: Norton, 2008).
3. See Joanna Macy and Molly Young Brown, *Coming Back to Life: Practices to Reconnect Our Lives, Our World* (Gabriola Island, BC: New Society Publishers, 1998).
4. Rebecca Solnit, *A Paradise Built in Hell: The Extraordinary Communities That Arise in Disaster* (New York: Viking, 2009), 10.
5. Rabindranath Tagore, *Gitanjali* (Brookline, MA: International Pocket Library, 1912), 45.

CHAPTER ONE. THREE STORIES OF OUR TIME

1. David Korten, *The Great Turning: From Empire to Earth Community* (Sterling, VA: Kumarian Press, 2006), 251.

2. George W. Bush, press briefing by Ari Fleischer, http://www.presidency
    .ucsb.edu/ws/index.php?pid=47520#axzz1VIT70S9z.

3. Rich Pirog and Andrew Benjamin, "Checking the Food Odometer:
    Comparing Food Miles for Local Versus Conventional Produce Sales to
    Iowa Institutions," Leopold Center for Sustainable Agriculture, 2003,
    http://www.leopold.iastate.edu/pubs-and-papers/2003-07-food-
    odometer.

4. "Obama at G20: U.S. Needs Faster Growth to Curb Deficit," *Reuters*,
    November 11, 2010, http://www.reuters.com/article/2010/11/11
    /us-obama-deficits-idUSTRE6AA20H20101111.

5. Anup Shah, "Children as Consumers," *Global Issues*, November 21, 2010,
    http://www.globalissues.org/article/237/children-as-consumers.

6. Oliver James, *Affluenza* (London: Vermillion, 2007), 81.

7. Paul Solman, "China's Vast Consumer Class," *PBS NewsHour*, http://
    www.pbs.org/newshour/bb/asia/july-dec05/consumers_10-05.html.

8. "Where America Stands: Economic Worries Persist; Dissatisfaction with
    Washington Runs High," *CBS News* poll, May 25, 2010, http://www.
    cbsnews.com/htdocs/pdf/poll_052510.pdf.

9. "57% Think Next Generation Will Be Worse Off," *Fox News* poll, April 9,
    2010, http://www.foxnews.com/politics/2010/04/09/fox-news-poll
    -think-generation-worse/.

10. "Global Survey Highlights Fear of Future and Lack of Faith in World
    Leaders," Gallup International Poll, January 17, 2008, http://extranet
    .gallup-international.com/uploads/internet/DAVOS%20release%20
    final.pdf.

11. Korten, *Great Turning*, 21.

12. Karen Ward, Zoe Knight, Nick Robins, Paul Spedding, and Charanjit
    Singh, "Energy in 2050: Will Fuel Constraints Thwart Our Growth
    Projections?" HSBC Global Research, March 2011, http://www.research
    .hsbc.com/midas/Res/RDV?p=pdf&key=TBouEyzId3&n=293253.PDF.

13. See Jeff Rubin, "Oil Prices Caused the Current Recession," *The Oil Drum*,
    November 5, 2008, http://www.theoildrum.com/node/4727.

14. See Rob Hopkins, *The Transition Handbook: From Oil Dependency to Local
    Resilience* (White River Junction, VT: Chelsea Green, 2008), 21–22.

15. "Coping with Water Scarcity: Challenge of Twenty-First Century,"
    World Water Day Report, 2007, http://www.fao.org/nr/water/docs
    /escarcity.pdf.

16. Albert Schumacher, "Water for All: Moving Towards Access to Fresh
    Drinking Water and Sanitation," *UN Chronicle*, 2005, http://www.un.org
    /Pubs/chronicle/2005/issue2/0205p20.html.

17. Aiguo Dai, Kevin E. Trenberth, and Taotao Qian, "A Global Dataset of Palmer Drought Severity Index for 1870–2002: Relationship with Soil Moisture and Effects of Surface Warming," *J. Hydrometeor* 5 (2004): 1117–30, doi: 10.1175/JHM-386.1.

18. Quoted in "Recycling Facts," *Green Muze*, August 21, 2008, http://www .greenmuze.com/waste/recycling/289-recycling-facts.html.

19. William J. Antholis and Martin S. Induk, "How We're Doing Compared with the Rest of the World," Brookings Institution, February 13, 2011, http://www.brookings.edu/papers/2011/0213_recovery_renewal.aspx.

20. For a detailed overview of how the world is warming, see "The State of the Climate Highlights, 2009," National Oceanic and Atmospheric Administration, July 2010, http://www1.ncdc.noaa.gov/pub/data/cmb /bams-sotc/2009/bams-sotc-2009-brochure-lo-rez.pdf.

21. Petra Low, "Weather-Related Disasters Dominate," Worldwatch Institute, October 1, 2008, http://vitalsigns.worldwatch.org/vs-trend/weather -related-disasters-dominate.

22. See reports on Climate Central, http://www.climatecentral.org/videos /web_features/washington_warming_and_wildfires.

23. Quoted in "Massive California Fires Consistent with Climate Change, Experts Say," *Science Daily*, October 24, 2007, http://www.sciencedaily .com/releases/2007/10/071024103856.htm.

24. Gordon McGranahan, Deborah Balk, and Bridget Anderson, "The Rising Tide: Assessing the Risks of Climate Change and Human Settlements in Low Elevation Coastal Zones," *Environment and Urbanization* 19 (2007): 17, doi: 10.1177/0956247807076960.

25. Tim Lenton, Anthony Footitt, and Andrew Dlugolecki, "Major Tipping Points in the Earth's Climate System and Consequences for the Insurance Sector," World Wildlife Fund/Allianz SE, November 23, 2009, http:// assets.panda.org/downloads/plugin_tp_final_report.pdf.

26. Quoted by Jenny Fyall, "Warming Will 'Wipe Out Billions,'" *The Scotsman*, November 29, 2009, http://news.scotsman.com/latestnews /Warming-will-39wipe-out-billions39.5867379.jp.

27. UN Food and Agriculture Organization Food Price Index, August 9, 2011, http://www.fao.org/worldfoodsituation/wfs-home/foodpricesindex /en/.

28. See Anup Shah, "Poverty Facts and Stats," *Global Issues*, September 20, 2010, http://www.globalissues.org/article/26/poverty-facts-and-stats.

29. Shah, "Poverty Facts."

30. Joseph Stiglitz, "Of the 1%, by the 1%, for the 1%," *Vanity Fair*, May 2011,

http://www.vanityfair.com/society/features/2011/05/top-one-percent
-201105.

31. Richard Wilkinson and Kate Pickett, *The Spirit Level: Why More Equal Societies Almost Always Do Better* (New York: Penguin, 2009).

32. Jeffrey Sachs, "Can Extreme Poverty Be Eliminated?: Crossroads for Poverty," *Scientific American* (September 2005): 56–65.

33. "World Military Spending Reached $1.6 Trillion in 2010," Stockholm International Peace Research Institute, April 11, 2011, http://www.sipri .org/media/pressreleases/milex.

34. "Global Biodiversity Outlook 2," Convention on Biological Diversity, 2006, http://www.cbd.int/doc/gbo/gbo2/cbd-gbo2-en.pdf.

35. Lauren Morello and ClimateWire, "Phytoplankton Population Drops 40 Percent Since 1950," *Scientific American*, July 29, 2010, http://www .scientificamerican.com/article.cfm?id=phytoplankton-population.

36. "Al Gore's New Thinking on the Climate Crisis," TED talk, March 2008, http://www.ted.com/talks/al_gore_s_new_thinking_on_the_climate _crisis.html.

37. See Hopkins, *Transition Handbook*, 26.

38. Donella H. Meadows, Jørgen Randers, and Dennis L. Meadows, *Limits to Growth: The 30-Year Update* (White River Junction, VT: Chelsea Green, 2004), 3.

39. Paul Hawken, *Blessed Unrest: How the Largest Movement in the World Came into Being and No One Saw It Coming* (New York: Penguin, 2008), 2.

40. "Economic Crisis Turns UK Customers to Ethical Banking, Savings, and Investments," NOP Poll for Triodos Bank, http://www.ethicalconsumer. org/CommentAnalysis/marketresearch/2009reports.aspx.

41. As quoted on Space Quotations, http://www.spacequotations.com/earth .html.

42. "Bill Anders," Wikipedia, last modified October 2, 2011, http://en .wikipedia.org/wiki/William_Anders.

CHAPTER THREE. COMING FROM GRATITUDE

1. Robert Emmons, "The Joy of Thanks," *Spirituality & Health* (Winter 2002), http://www.spiritualityhealth.com/magazine/recommended -articles/the-joy-of-thanks.html.

2. Reviewed in Emily Polak and Michael McCullough, "Is Gratitude an Alternative to Materialism?" *Journal of Happiness Studies* 7, no. 3 (2006): 343–60, doi: 10.1007/s10902-005-3649-5.

3. R. A. Emmons and M. E. McCullough, "Counting Blessings Versus

Burdens: An Experimental Investigation of Gratitude and Subjective Well-Being in Daily Life," *Journal of Personality and Social Psychology*, 84, no. 2 (2003): 377–89, doi: 10.1037/0022-3514.84.2.377.

4. Michael E. McCullough, Marcia B. Kimeldorf, and Adam D. Cohen, "An Adaptation for Altruism? The Social Causes, Social Effects, and Social Evolution of Gratitude," *Current Directions in Psychological Science* 17, no. 4 (2008): 281–85, http://www.psy.miami.edu/ehblab/Gratitude /Gratitude_CDPS_2008.pdf.

5. Alice Isen and Paula Levin, "Effect of Feeling Good on Helping: Cookies and Kindness," *Journal of Personality and Social Psychology* 21, no. 3 (1972): 384–388, doi: 10.1037/h0032317.

6. Polak and McCullough, "Gratitude," 347.

7. Oliver James, *Affluenza* (London: Vermillion, 2007), 28.

8. See Oliver James, *Britain on the Couch: Treating a Low-Serotonin Society* (London: Arrow, 1998), 96–110.

9. A. E. Becker et al., "Eating Behaviour and Attitudes Following Prolonged Exposure to Television Among Ethnic Fijian Adolescent Girls," *British Journal of Psychiatry* 180 (2002): 509–14, doi: 10.1192/bjp.180.6.509.

10. Jerry Bader, "The Law of Dissatisfaction: How to Motivate Prospects," *Woodridge Marketing Articles*, http://www.mrpwebmedia.com/blog /the-law-of-dissatisfaction-how-to-motivate-prospects.

11. Explored in detail by Gregg Easterbrook in *The Progress Paradox: How Life Gets Better While People Feel Worse* (New York: Random House, 2004).

12. Gavin Andrews, Richie Poulton, and Ingmar Skoog, "Lifetime Risk of Depression: Restricted to a Minority or Waiting for Most?" *British Journal of Psychiatry* 187 (2005): 495–96.

13. Environmental Protection Agency, "Sustainable Materials Management: The Road Ahead" (Washington, DC: EPA, 2009), 2, http://www.epa .gov/osw/inforesources/pubs/vision2.pdf.

14. T. Kasser, R. M. Ryan, C. E. Couchman, and K. M. Sheldon, "Materialistic Values: Their Causes and Consequences," in *Psychology and Consumer Culture: The Struggle for a Good Life in a Materialistic World*, ed. T. Kasser and A. D. Kanner (Washington, DC: American Psychological Association, 2004), 11–28.

15. Polak and McCullough, "Gratitude," 356.

16. See Richard Layard, *Happiness: Lessons from a New Science* (New York: Penguin, 2005), 81.

17. See "A Basic Call to Consciousness: The Haudenosaunee Address to the Western World," *Akwesasne Notes* (1978), http://ratical.org/many_ worlds/6Nations/6nations1.html#part1.

18. The Thanksgiving Address is viewable at http://www.nmai.si.edu
    /education/files/thanksgiving_address.pdf.
19. See "The Tree of Peace," *Native American Wisdom*, http://www.earth
    portals.com/Portal_Messenger/shenandoah.html.
20. James Lovelock, *Healing Gaia: Practical Medicine for the Planet* (New York:
    Harmony Books, 1991), 113.
21. Lovelock, *Healing Gaia*, 22.
22. Lovelock, *Healing Gaia*, 133.
23. Paying it forward is a powerful concept, beautifully illustrated in the film
    Pay It Forward, directed by Mimi Leder (2000).

CHAPTER FOUR. HONORING OUR PAIN FOR THE WORLD

1. The version used here is based on Joanna's translation of the thirteenth-
   century poem by Wolfram von Eschenbach.
2. Bibb Latané and John Darley, "Group Inhibition of Bystander Intervention
   in Emergencies," *Journal of Personality and Social Psychology* 10, no. 3
   (1968): 215–21.
3. See Paul Farhi, "Liberal Media Watchdog: Fox News E-Mail Shows
   Network's Slant on Climate Change," *Washington Post*, December 15, 2010,
   http://www.washingtonpost.com/wp-dyn/content/article/2010/12/15
   /AR2010121503181.html.
4. See Sutin Wannabovorn, "Thai Meteorology Chief Who Got It Right Is
   Brought In from the Cold," *Guardian*, January 12, 2005,
   http://www.guardian.co.uk/world/2005/jan/12/tsunami2004.thailand.
5. See Naomi Oreskes and Erik Conway, *Merchants of Doubt: How a Handful
   of Scientists Obscured the Truth on Issues from Tobacco Smoke to Global
   Warming* (New York: Bloomsbury Press, 2010).
6. See Cassandra Larussa, "BP Enjoys Lobbying Strength, Close Ties to
   Lawmakers as Federal Investigation Looms," OpenSecrets, April 30, 2010,
   http://www.opensecrets.org/news/2010/04/on-thursday-oil-giant-bp
   .html.
7. "World Troubles Affect Parenthood," BBC News, October 8, 2007,
   http://news.bbc.co.uk/1/hi/uk/7033102.stm.
8. For a follow-up study of outcomes in participants, see Chris Johnstone,
   "Reconnecting with Our World," in *Creative Advances in Groupwork*, ed.
   Anna Chesner and Herb Hahn (London: Jessica Kingsley, 2002).
9. While initially developed in relation to death and dying, the Kübler-Ross
   model of denial, anger, bargaining, depression, and acceptance is now more
   widely applied to the process of coming to terms with any kind of loss. See
   Elisabeth Kübler-Ross and David Kessler, *On Grief and Grieving: Finding*

the Meaning of Grief through the Five Stages of Loss (New York: Scribner, 2005).

10.   J. William Worden, *Grief Counseling and Grief Therapy: A Handbook for the Mental Health Practitioner*, 4th ed. (New York: Springer Publishing, 2008).

11.   Quoted in Joanna Macy and Molly Young Brown, *Coming Back to Life: Practices to Reconnect Our Lives, Our World* (Gabriola Island, BC: New Society Publishers, 1998), 91.

12.   Arne Naess, "The Shallow and the Deep, Long-Range Ecology Movement," *Inquiry* 16, nos. 1–4 (1973): 95–100, doi: 10.1080 /00201747308601682.

13.   Margaret Wheatley, "Dear Friends and Colleagues," *Turning to One Another*, http://www.turningtooneanother.net/home.html.

CHAPTER FIVE. A WIDER SENSE OF SELF

1.   Arne Naess, "Self-Realization: An Ecological Approach to Being in the World," in *Thinking Like a Mountain: Toward a Council of All Beings*, ed. John Seed, Joanna Macy, Pat Fleming, and Arne Naess (Kalispell, MT: Heretic Books, 1988), 28–29.

2.   Sam Keen, from "Hymns to an Unknown God," in *The Sacred Earth: Writers on Nature and Spirit*, ed. Jason Gardner (Novato, CA: New World Library, 1998), 122.

3.   Helena Norberg-Hodge, *Ancient Futures: Learning from Ladakh*, 2nd ed. (London: Rider, 2000), 83.

4.   Carl Jung, "Spirit and Life," in *The Collected Works of C. G. Jung*, vol. 8, *The Structure and Dynamics of the Psyche* (London: Routledge & Kegan Paul, 1960), 337.

5.   Naess, "Self-Realization," 28.

6.   Marilynn Brewer, "The Social Self: On Being the Same and Different at the Same Time," *Personality and Social Psychology Bulletin* 17, no. 5 (1991): 476, doi: 10.1177/0146167291175001.

7.   Described by Naess in "Self-Realization," 28.

8.   World Values Survey, quoted by Robert Putnam, *Bowling Alone: The Collapse and Revival of American Community* (New York: Simon & Schuster, 2000), 140.

9.   Naess, "Self-Realization," 20.

10.   Quoted in Joanna Macy, *World as Lover, World as Self* (Berkeley, CA: Parallax Press, 2007), 150.

11.   Harvey Sindima, "Community of Life: Ecological Theology in African Perspective," in *Liberating Life: Contemporary Approaches in Ecological Theology*, ed. Charles Birch, William Eaken, and Jay B. McDaniel (New

York: Orbis, 1990), xx, http://www.religion-online.org/showarticle.
asp?title=2327.

12. For more on this story, see Wes McKinley and Caron Balkany, *The Ambushed Grand Jury: How the Justice Department Covered Up Government Nuclear Crimes and How We Caught Them Red Handed* (Lanham, MD: Apex Press, 2004).

13. Wes McKinley in video interview, Wes McKinley and Caron Balkany, *The Ambushed Grand Jury*, http://www.ambushedgrandjury.com/video.htm.

14. Quoted in Wes McKinley & Caron Balkany, *The Ambushed Grand Jury* (New York, Apex Press, 2004), 165.

15. Lynn Margulis and Dorion Sagan, *Microcosmos: Four Billion Years of Evolution from Our Microbial Ancestors* (Berkeley and Los Angeles: University of California Press, 1997), 29.

CHAPTER SIX. A DIFFERENT KIND OF POWER

1. "World Troubles Affect Parenthood," *BBC News*, October 8, 2007, http://news.bbc.co.uk/1/hi/uk/7033102.stm.

2. Joe Litobarski, "We Are Powerless to Stop Climate Change," *Th!nk About It*, November 14, 2009, http://climatechange.thinkaboutit.eu/think4/post/we_are_powerless_to_stop_climate_change.

3. "World Military Spending Reached $1.6 Trillion in 2010," Stockholm International Peace Research Institute, April 11, 2011, http://www.sipri.org/media/pressreleases/milex.

4. Jeffrey Sachs, "Can Extreme Poverty Be Eliminated?: Crossroads for Poverty," *Scientific American* (September 2005): 56–65.

5. Nelson Mandela, *Long Walk to Freedom: The Autobiography of Nelson Mandela* (London: Abacus, 1995), 625.

6. D. H. Lawrence, "The Third Thing," *Pansies: Poems* (Knopf, 1929), 133.

7. Mandela, *Long Walk*, 438.

8. Joanna Macy, "Grace and the Great Turning," The Co-Intelligence Institute, http://www.co-intelligence.org/Grace_Macy.html.

9. Quoted in Joanna Macy, *Despair and Personal Power in the Nuclear Age* (Gabriola Island, BC: New Society Publishers, 1983), 134. Adapted from T. H. White, *The Sword in the Stone* (New York: Putnam, 1939).

CHAPTER SEVEN. A RICHER EXPERIENCE OF COMMUNITY

1. M. Scott Peck, *The Different Drum: Community Making and Peace* (London: Arrow, 1990), 27.

2. Miller McPherson, Lynn Smith-Lovin, and Matthew Brashears, "Social Isolation in America," *American Sociological Review* 71, no. 3 (June 2006): 353–75.

3. Robert Putnam, *Bowling Alone: The Collapse and Revival of American Community* (New York: Simon & Schuster, 2000).

4. "Better Together," Saguaro Seminar report, December 2000, 10, http://www.bettertogether.org/thereport.htm.

5. Rebecca Solnit, *A Paradise Built in Hell: The Extraordinary Communities That Arise in Disaster* (New York: Viking, 2009), 3–4.

6. Solnit, *Paradise*, 5.

7. Doris Haddock, "Fear Is a Humbug," *New Hampshire* magazine (December 1, 2008), http://www.nhmagazine.com/archives/404336-329/fear-is-a-humbug.html.

8. See Joanna Macy, *Dharma and Development: Religion as Resource in the Sarvodaya Self-Help Movement*, rev. ed. (Sterling, VA: Kumarian Press, 1991).

9. "Action Handbook: Ideas for Transition Projects," Transition United States, http://www.transitionus.org/sites/default/files/HowTo_ActionHandbook_v1%200.pdf.

10. Martin Luther King Jr., "Letter from Birmingham Jail," April 16, 1963, paragraph 4, http://abacus.bates.edu/admin/offices/dos/mlk/letter.html.

11. Every day 29,000 children under the age of five die from preventable diseases, malnutrition being a contributing factor in more than half of these. See "Childhood under Threat: The State of the World's Children," Unicef, 2005, 9, http://www.unicef.org/sowc05/english/fullreport.html.

12. Donella Meadows, "If the World Were a Village of 1,000 People," Squidoo, http://www.squidoo.com/world-village-1000-people.

13. See http://www.odt.org/popvillagesources.htm.

14. Helena Norberg-Hodge, "The Pressure to Modernise," International Society for Ecology and Culture, 1992, http://www.localfutures.org/publications/online-articles/the-pressure-to-modernise.

15. Helena Norberg-Hodge, *Ancient Futures: Learning from Ladakh*, 2nd ed. (London: Rider, 2000), 45.

16. See Molly McNulty, "She's Swimming the Skeena," Skeena Watershed Conservation Coalition, August 5, 2009, http://skeenawatershed.com/news/article/shes_swimming_the_skeena/.

17. James Lovelock, *The Vanishing Face of Gaia: A Final Warning* (New York: Allen Lane, 2009), 9.

18. See Mohawk Nation, "Thanksgiving Prayer," http://www.mohawkcommunity.com/images/Thanksgving_prayer_1_.pdf.

19. See International Union for Conservation of Nature, "IUCN Redlist," http://www.iucnredlist.org.

20. Duane Elgin, *Promise Ahead: A Vision of Hope and Action for Humanity's Future* (North Yorkshire, UK: Quill, 2001), 28.

21. See Pat Fleming and Joanna Macy, "The Council of All Beings," in *Thinking Like a Mountain: Toward a Council of All Beings*, ed. John Seed, Joanna Macy, Pat Fleming, and Arne Naess (Kalispell, MT: Heretic Books, 1988), 79–90.

CHAPTER EIGHT. A LARGER VIEW OF TIME

1. See GRID-Arendal, United Nations Environmental Program, "Collapse of Atlantic Cod Stocks off the East Coast of Newfoundland in 1992," http://maps.grida.no/go/graphic/collapse-of-atlantic-cod-stocks-off-the-east-coast-of-newfoundland-in-1992.

2. Boris Worm et al., "Impacts of Biodiversity Loss on Ocean Ecosystem Services," *Science* 314 (2006): 787–90, doi: 10.1126/science.1132294.

3. "Market Crisis 'Will Happen Again,'" BBC News, September 8, 2009, http://news.bbc.co.uk/1/hi/8244600.stm.

4. "Quant Trading: How Mathematicians Rule the Markets," BBC News, September 26 2011, http://www.bbc.co.uk/news/business-14631547.

5. Quoted in Jem Bendell and Jonathan Cohen, "World Review," *Journal of Corporate Citizenship*, no. 27 (June 2007): 10.

6. See Greg Palast, *The Best Democracy Money Can Buy* (London: Robinson, 2003), 257.

7. National Commission on the BP Deepwater Horizon Oil Spill and Offshore Drilling, "Deep Water: The Gulf Oil Disaster and the Future of Offshore Drilling," Report to the President (January 2011), 125, http://www.gpoaccess.gov/deepwater/index.html.

8. "Deep Water," 125.

9. Gordon McGranahan, Deborah Balk, and Bridget Anderson, "The Rising Tide: Assessing the Risks of Climate Change and Human Settlements in Low Elevation Coastal Zones," *Environment and Urbanization* 19 (2007): 17, doi: 10.1177/0956247807076960.

10. See "Lake Karachay," Wikipedia, last updated August 18, 2011, http://en.wikipedia.org/wiki/Lake_Karachay.

11. Malidoma Patrice Somé, *Of Water and the Spirit: Ritual, Magic, and Initiation in the Life of an African Shaman* (New York: Penguin, 1994), 9.

12. Several sources were used for this. For an overview, see "Timeline of Evolution," Wikipedia, last updated October 2, 2011, http://en.wikipedia.org/wiki/Timeline_of_evolution.

13. Several sources were used for this. For an overview, see "Timeline of Ancient History," Wikipedia, last updated October 1, 2011. http://en.wikipedia.org/wiki/Timeline_of_ancient_history.

14. Jared Diamond, *Collapse: How Societies Choose to Fail or Survive* (New York: Penguin, 2006), 495.

15. This exercise is adapted from the Double Circle process described in Joanna Macy and Molly Young Brown, *Coming Back to Life: Practices to Reconnect Our Lives, Our World* (Gabriola Island, BC: New Society Publishers, 1998), 146.

Chapter Nine. Catching an Inspiring Vision

1. The full speech is available at Martin Luther King Online, http://www.mlkonline.net.

2. Elise Boulding, "Turning Walls into Doorways," *Inward Light* 47, no. 101 (spring 1986), http://fcrp.quaker.org/InwardLight101/101Boulding.html.

3. Jill Bolte Taylor, a neuroanatomist who suffered a stroke, combines her personal experience with neuroscience research in describing the different roles of our two cerebral hemispheres. See *My Stroke of Insight: A Brain Scientist's Personal Journey* (New York: Penguin, 2009).

4. Stephen Covey, *The Seven Habits of Highly Effective People* (New York: Simon & Schuster, 1990), 99.

5. Boulding, "Turning Walls."

6. Ibid.

7. See Coleman Barks, trans., *The Essential Rumi* (San Francisco: HarperSanFrancisco, 1995).

8. See J. Edward Russo and Paul Schoemaker, *Confident Decision Making: How to Make the Right Decision Every Time* (London: Piatkus, 1991), 111.

9. Thomas Berry, *The Dream of the Earth* (San Francisco: Sierra Club Books, 1990), 201.

10. See the Co-Intelligence Institute, http://www.co-intelligence.org/I-wholeness.html.

11. Joseph Campbell, *The Hero's Journey: Joseph Campbell on His Life and Work* (Novato, CA: New World Library, 2003), 217.

Chapter Ten. Daring to Believe It Is Possible

1. Quoted in Ellen Gibson Wilson, *Thomas Clarkson: A Biography* (New York: Macmillan, 1989), 11.

2. Described most movingly in Adam Hochschild, *Bury the Chains: The British Struggle to Abolish Slavery* (London: Pan McMillan, 2006).

3. Joseph Campbell, *The Hero with a Thousand Faces* (1949; repr., n.p.: Fontana, 1993), 92.

4. The origin of this quote is thought to be a combination of Goethe and W. H. Murray. See Goethe Society of North America, "Popular Quotes: Commitment," http://www.goethesociety.org/pages/quotescom.html.

CHAPTER ELEVEN. BUILDING SUPPORT AROUND YOU

1. Paul Ray and Sherry Ruth Anderson, *The Cultural Creatives: How 50 Million People Are Changing the World* (New York: Harmony Books, 2000), 44.
2. P. W. Schultz et al., "The Constructive, Destructive, and Reconstructive Power of Social Norms," *Psychological Science* 18 (2007): 429–34.
3. Described in David Gershon, *Social Change* 2.0: A Blueprint for Reinventing Our World (White River Junction, VT: Chelsea Green, 2009).
4. Interviewed by Chris Johnstone, "Changing the World from Your Neighbourhood," *Permaculture* magazine (March 7, 2011), http://www.permaculture.co.uk/articles/changing-world-your-neighbourhood.
5. Cecily Maller et al., "Healthy Nature, Healthy People: 'Contact with Nature' as an Upstream Health Promotion Intervention for Populations," *Health Promotion International* 21, no. 1 (December 2005): 45–54, doi: 10.1093/heapro/dai032.

CHAPTER TWELVE. MAINTAINING ENERGY AND ENTHUSIASM

1. See Bob Abernethy, "Profile: Frederick Buechner," *Religion & Ethics Newsweekly*, online newsletter, episode no. 936, May 5, 2006, http://www.pbs.org/wnet/religionandethics/week936/profile.html.
2. Mihaly Csikszentmihalyi, *Flow: The Psychology of Happiness* (London: Rider, 1992), 3.
3. See, for example, Action for Happiness, http://www.actionforhappiness.org. See also Helena Norberg-Hodge's film *The Economics of Happiness* (2011).
4. See links at Chris Johnstone, "Happiness Lectures," http://www.chrisjohnstone.info/happiness_lectures.htm.
5. John Robbins, *The New Good Life: Living Better Than Ever in an Age of Less* (New York: Ballantine, 2010), 5.
6. Robbins, *New Good Life*, 10.
7. John Robbins, *Diet for a New America*, 2nd ed. (Walpole, NH: Stillpoint, 1998).
8. Robbins, *New Good Life*, xv.

9. See Bioregional Development Group and WWF International, One Planet Living, http://www.oneplanetliving.org.

Chapter Thirteen. Strengthened by Uncertainty

1. Jared Diamond, *Collapse: How Societies Choose to Fail or Survive* (New York: Penguin, 2006), 498.
2. Boris Cyrulnik, *Resilience: How Your Inner Strength Can Set You Free from the Past* (New York: Penguin, 2009), 286.

Resources

We have set up a website at activehope.info to offer additional materials, a guide for study-action groups, and information about resources to complement this book. We include here some of our favorites, with ten websites, ten books, and five resources for study action groups.

Ten Websites

celdf.org

Information about a new rights-based approach to protection from corporate plundering. The Community Environmental Legal Defense Fund and its "Democracy Schools" offer new ideas and legal tools for local action.

facilitationforlifeonearth.org

UK-based workshops and facilitator training in the Work That Reconnects and Inner Transition.

greatturningtimes.org

Set up and coedited by Chris, this site offers a free email newsletter and web resources to support our participation in the Great Turning.

joannamacy.net

Background on Joanna's work and thought, as well as her current teaching schedule.

livingeconomiesforum.org

David Korten's latest commentaries on the Great Turning, with a focus on the emergence of a new economy.

nirs.org

For people and organizations concerned about nuclear power and radioactive pollution, the Nuclear Information and Resource Service offers excellent reporting, networking, and renewable energy links.

theworkthatreconnects.org

An online video resource for practical orientation to the Work That Reconnects, featuring Joanna's reflections and demonstrations (also available as a DVD).

transitionculture.org

A blog by Rob Hopkins with the latest news on how Transition Initiatives are spreading and building resilience for a postcarbon era.

vandanashiva.org

An entrée into the world of Vandana Shiva, India's brilliant, outspoken scientist-activist, defender of our planet's agricultural and food systems.

yesmagazine.org

For a lively panorama of adventures in the Great Turning.

TEN BOOKS

Thomas Berry, *Evening Thoughts: Reflecting on Earth as Sacred Community*. This culminating collection of essays from Thomas Berry not only provides all the arguments we need for Active Hope, but it is also a hymn to the beauty and power of the vision we can awaken to.

Jonathan Dawson, Ross Jackson, and Helena Norberg-Hodge, eds. *Gaian Economics: Living Well within Planetary Limits*. This rich and engaging collection, brimming with practicality, is one of four volumes in the Four Keys to the Design of Sustainable Communities series. This series is produced by international teams, reflecting a partnership between eco-villages and the United Nations. The other titles in the series are *Beyond You and Me: Inspirations and Wisdom for Building Community*; *The Song of the Earth: A Synthesis of Scientific and Spiritual Worldviews*; and *Designing Ecological Habitats: Creating a Sense of Place*.

David Gershon, *Social Change 2.0: A Blueprint for Reinventing Our World*. Offers inspiring case studies that illustrate community-empowerment principles and tools.

Richard Heinberg, *The End of Growth: Adapting to Our New Economic Reality*. Here the delusion that animates Business as Usual and still maintains an iron grip on politicians and financiers is unmasked — an essential step toward getting clear on where we are and where we can go.

Rob Hopkins, *The Transition Handbook: From Oil Dependency to Local Resilience*. Introduces the concepts of Transition and peak oil, exploring the "head, heart, and hands" of change.

Ellen LaConte, *Life Rules: Why So Much Is Going Wrong Everywhere at Once and How Life Teaches Us to Fix It*. A homesteader who walks her talk, LaConte helps us learn from the ultimate teacher and law giver if we want to understand both the peril and the promise of our time.

Winona LaDuke, *All My Relations*. An Anishinaabe spokesperson, as well as vice presidential candidate for the Green Party in 1996 and 2000, LaDuke show how an understanding of the Native American experience and spirituality is essential to our future. This message is amplified in her subsequent book *Recovering the Sacred: The Power of Naming and Reclaiming*.

Nelson Mandela, *A Long Walk to Freedom*. We need stories that offer us models of commitment, compassion, endurance, and resilience. Nelson Mandela's autobiography is one such story.

John Robbins, *The New Good Life*. From the author of *Diet for a New America* comes a welcome counterpoint to consumerism, with a guide to a good life that doesn't cost the Earth.

Rebecca Solnit, *A Paradise Built in Hell*. A graphic portrayal of the social possibilities revealed in our responses to disaster, describing how the best can be drawn out of us.

GUIDES FOR STUDY ACTION GROUPS

bethechangeearthalliance.org

See the Action Circles pages under the programs section for guidance on setting up study action groups/circles, and the Action Guide in the products section for a wonderful supporting resource.

earth-circles.org

Here are guidelines for drawing groups together to learn about the challenges of climate change and respond creatively with lifestyle choices and political action.

localcircles.org

Also known as Resilience Circles, Common Security Clubs bring neighbors together to foster community, mutual support, and understanding of economic realities in an ongoing and deepening recession.

localfutures.org

An online service of the Institute for Study of Ecology and Culture, this website offers place-based knowledge and contacts for data assessment and local action.

nwei.org

The Northwest Earth Institute offers guidelines and readings tailored to eight-session discussion groups on topics such as deep ecology, voluntary simplicity, and corporate globalization.

Index

B

banks, 29–30
"Basic Call to Consciousness"
  (Haudenosaunee document), 50,
  51, 53
Berry, Thomas, 175
biodiversity, 93
Blessed Unrest (Hawken), 27
bodhichitta, 100, 217, 225, 227, 233
Bodhisattva Perspective, The
  (exercise), 234–37
bodhisattvas, 101, 233–37
Boulding, Elise, 164, 169–71
boycotts, 28
BP Macondo oil spill (2010), 147
brainstorming, progressive,
  177–78, 224–25
Breathing Through (exercise),
  73–75, 78
Brever, Jacque, 95–97
Brewer, Marilynn, 91
Bristol Happiness Lectures, 220
British Medical Association, 196,
  197
Buddhism, 66–67, 73, 100–103,
  226–27
    See also *bodhichitta*; bodhisatt-
    vas; interconnectedness
Buechner, Frederick, 218–19
burnout, 213, 214, 216
Bush, George W., 13–14
Business as Usual
  assumptions behind, 4–5, 16,
    122
  attractions of, 14–15
  challenges to, 187
  community and, 129

consumption as viewed in, 157
global spread of, 16–17
gratitude as viewed in, 50–51,
  53
Great Unraveling vs., 24–26
individualism in, 50–51, 61
narrow timescapes of, 149,
  152, 211
plot/subplots of, 15, 122
privatization in, 52–53
success as viewed in, 223–24
survival response and, 59–60,
  61
uncertainty and, 229, 232
as unsustainable, 8, 13–14, 146

C

cairn of mourning, 79
Campbell, Joseph, 179, 191
cancer, 126
CBS polls, 17
ceremony, 79
change, discontinuous, 187, 189–91
Clarkson, Thomas, 185, 186, 187
climate change
  blocked response to, 60–61
  Business as Usual and, 5
  deforestation and, 55
  disasters resulting from, 126,
    147
  discouraging facts concerning,
    186
  extreme weather events result-
    ing from, 25
  fears concerning, 1
  gratitude and, 56

About the Authors

Ecophilosopher Joanna Macy, Ph.D., is a scholar of Buddhism, general systems theory, and deep ecology. A respected voice in the movements for peace, justice, and ecology, she interweaves her scholarship with five decades of activism. As the root teacher of the Work That Reconnects, she has created a groundbreaking theoretical framework for personal and social change, as well as a powerful workshop methodology for its application.

Her wide-ranging work addresses psychological and spiritual issues of the nuclear age, the cultivation of ecological awareness, and the fruitful resonance between Buddhist thought and contemporary science. The many dimensions of this work are explored in her books and DVD.

Many people around the world have participated in Joanna's workshops and trainings. Her group methods, known as the Work That Reconnects, have been adopted and adapted yet more widely in classrooms, churches, and grassroots organizing. Her work helps people transform despair and apathy, in the face of overwhelming social and ecological crises, into constructive, collaborative action. It brings a new way of seeing the world as our larger living body, freeing us from the assumptions and attitudes that now threaten the continuity of life on Earth.

Joanna travels widely, giving lectures, workshops, and trainings in the Americas, Europe, Asia, and Australia. She lives in Berkeley,

California, near her children and grandchildren. Her website is at
joannamacy.net.

Chris Johnstone is a medical doctor, author, and coach who worked
for nearly twenty years as an addictions specialist in the UK National Health Service. A former Senior Teaching Fellow at Bristol
University Medical School, he trains health professionals in behavioral medicine and leads courses exploring the psychological
dimensions of planetary crisis. Chris is known for his work pio-
neering the role of resilience training in promoting positive mental health, developing self-help resources and setting up the Bristol
Happiness Lectures. He is author of *Find Your Power: A Toolkit for
Resilience and Positive Change* (2010) and co-presenter of *The Happiness Training Plan* CD (2010).

Chris has been a trainer in the Work That Reconnects for more
than two decades, working with Joanna on many occasions and running facilitator trainings in the United Kingdom. In 2004 he set up
the free email newsletter called *The Great Turning Times*, which
is now read by thousands of people throughout the world. He has
been active in the Transition movement since its very beginnings
and contributed to a chapter on the psychology of change in *The
Transition Handbook* by Rob Hopkins.

After many years living in Bristol, Chris recently moved to the
North of Scotland, where he lives with his wife, Kirsty, and their
dogs and chickens, pursuing his love of growing fruit in their evolving forest garden. He continues his coaching and training work, as
well as his writing and music. His website is at chrisjohnstone.info.

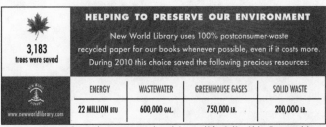